CW00554123

The Echo of a

Fighting Flower

The story of HMS Narcissus and B3 Ocean Escort Group in WWII

Dustcover: *Itchen* attacks U-666: *Narcissus* in foreground.
(Painted by Terry Rogers, ex-*HMS Bergamot,* based on a design by the author and owner)

The Echo of a Fighting Flower

The Story of HMS Narcissus and B3 Ocean Escort Group in WWII

Peter Coy

A SQUARE ONE PUBLICATION

First published in 1997 by
Square One Publications,
The Tudor House
Upton upon Severn, Worcs. WR8 0HT

© 1997 Peter Coy
ISBN 1 899955 22 4

British Library Cataloguing in Publication Data
is available for this title

Typeset in Palatino 11.5 on 13 by Avon Dataset Ltd, Bidford-on-Avon, Warwickshire, B50 4JH
Printed by Antony Rowe Ltd, Chippenham, Wilts

In memory of Gilbert and Ella

Acknowledgements

In respect of anecdotal evidence I am greatly indebted to the following for information and/or confirmation: Messrs Alwyn Davies, Gordon Drew, Aled Eames, John Esslemont (ex-*Balsam* for the photograph of U-boat pens), Alan Galloway and Clive Hall, all ex-Royal Navy; also to Messieurs Maurice Jacon and Pierre Perdraut (who has permitted his account of the Gibraltar fiasco to be quoted in full), both ex-Free French Navy. For the lead into Admiralty records I am very grateful to Mr Walter Ireland, MBE, for directing me towards the Naval Historical Branch in the MoD; the keeper of the German U-boat diaries there, Mr R M Coppock, who made me aware of the existence of a printed summary of the service of *Narcissus* by a Mr R A Ruegg of Walmer, who was kind enough to send me a copy. This listed the code number of every convoy she had escorted. From there it was a relatively simple task to raise every file in the PRO Kew relating to these convoys.

I am also grateful for the personal help of the author, J B Lamb, ex-Royal Canadian Naval Volunteer Reserve, of Derek Lukin–Johnston, also ex-RCNVR, of Dr Marc Milner of the University of New Brunswick and of Professor Dr Jürgen Rohwer, Stuttgart. Finally, I am much beholden to Mary Wilkinson for cleaning up my maps and diagrams.

I owe, of course, an obligation to the many post-War authors and publishers whose works I hope to have acknowledged adequately in the reference lists. Where I have made a few, short, direct quotations to reinforce my argument. I trust that their 'quality' can be perceived and that they are seen not to be 'substantial'.

And last, by no way least, I am grateful to Geny, for putting up with the stresses of research over three years.

Contents

	Foreword	ix
Chapter 1	Introduction	1
Chapter 2	Brothers-in-Arms: particularly the Canadians, Free French, Polish and Merchant Navies	21
Chapter 3	B3 Escort Group acquires HMS NARCISSUS for a succession of short convoys to the Mid-Ocean Meeting Point	39
Chapter 4	The Summer Respite of 1942 seven transocean convoys	59
Chapter 5	The Winter of 1942/43 Four B3 convoys between December and February; plus HX222 and SC117	79
Chapter 6	Convoy HX228 and the Lost Leader	95
Chapter 7	Convoy HX232 and the trials of AZALEA; NARCISSUS heads for Freetown	113
Chapter 8	A Pyrrhic 'victory' which turned the tide; the appearance of a new torpedo	129
Chapter 9	Farewell to the North Atlantic	145
Chapter 10	The Gibraltar Convoys: trailing our coat across the Bay of Biscay	153
Chapter 11	A Taste of 'Tobermory' and Farewell to B3 Group	169
Chapter 12	The Last Act: Normandy; and NARCISSUS arrives off Gold beach in the afternoon of D-Day	183
	Conclusion	195
	Bibliography	203
	Index	205

List of Illustrations

Fig. 1 HMS Narcissus   9
Fig. 2 Convoys Escorted by B3 Across the North Atlantic   20
Fig. 3 North Atlantic Ocean Termini & Hazards   58
Fig. 4 The Approximate Track of Convoy HX228   109
Fig. 5 The Classic Convoy Defence System   112
Fig. 6 Pyrrhic Victory   144

Royal Navy College, Greenwich   36
Induction Course of March 1942
German Enigma Coding Machine   37
Norwegian Survivors on board *Narcissus*
HMS Trawler *Northern Sky*
CAMShip   61
1942 Officers   74
Officer of the Watch   75
Forecastle covered in frozen spray
Pancake ice on open sea 1942/43   92
Port side forward, covered in snow
Amidships covered in snow   93
Forepart of *Narcissus* taken from the crow's nest
Afterpart of *Narcissus* taken from the crow's nest   94
German U-boat shelters in La Pallice today   110
HMS Azalea in April 1943 with convoy HX232   117
Narcissus & Orchis in Gibraltar
Signalmen using Aldis Lamp   127
HMCS *Iroquois*
Plum O'Reilly, our South African Engineer   180
The Second Captain with 2 Engineer Officers   181
Formal portrait of the crew 1944
Formal portrait of officers 1944   182
The graves of two *Orchis* casualties at Ryes, Normandy   189
Adml Horton, Cdr Evans, Lt Cdr Levasseur of *Aconit*   200
Horton with Capt Roberts & Cdr Evans   201
Post-War Reunion of B3 Group 1946/47   202

Foreword

Allied historians have variously ascribed the eventual Allied success in the Battle of the Atlantic to code-breaking (with particular reference to the well-kept Enigma/Ultra secret), to improved technological equipment (mainly the introduction of Radar and High Frequency Direction Finding), and to closing the mid-Atlantic gap in air cover for convoys (by constructing escort carriers and by wresting long-distance aircraft from Bomber Command).

The Germans, on the other hand, have sought an explanation for their failure to cut the trans-Atlantic lifeline in Hitler's paranoia: he kept on sending the U-boats off to what Dönitz regarded as the sideshows of, first, the Mediterranean theatre and, then, of a feared Allied invasion of Norway.

All of this reasoning has stimulated numerical speculation: what if, for example, Bletchley Park had not been able to decipher U-boat location signals and, therefore, the Admiralty had not been able to divert convoys away from danger? How many more shiploads of food, supplies and munitions would have been lost? What if, on the German side, U-boats had always been sent where the German admirals deemed their employment to be most profitable, instead of in pursuit of perceptions based upon Hitler's intuition?

The calculations produced by this type of speculation seem to have explained more convincingly the defeat of the U-boats than does the apparently ephemeral power of culture. In the end, however, such quantitative data remain purely speculative; the perceived qualitative differences between the human antagonists can always claim to have an equal influence upon the Battle outcome.

The degrees of skill and determination of contestants can be appraised after the event by the descriptions of participants; and the social context of war has always had its contemporary literary expression, whether in the Bayeux Tapestry to justify the defeat of the Saxons, or in the memoirs of Wellington's foot-soldiers to flesh out the Peninsular campaign. Such narratives often take the form of subjective accounts and the day-to-day concerns of ordinary individuals.

Two difficulties have stood in the way of personal reports on the Battle of the Atlantic: one was an absolute ban on the keeping of diaries; the other has been a disinclination to disclose recent instances of human frailty, despite the fact that these are normally as relevant as occasions of derring-do. The official prohibition of diaries appears only to have been obeyed by the now-indignant conformist: Nicholas Montsarrat of *Cruel Sea* fame was observed at the wardroom table, 'writing another of his books'; Admiral Tomkinson, the 'Invergordon Scapegoat', is described as having 'written peevishly in his diary – the keeping of which by officers was banned by the Admiralty...'.[1] The junior officer expresses his worm's eye view into fictional sea-stories; the senior officer either has his biographer or himself writes loftily of the higher strategies. Who can now doubt that both have depended heavily upon their diaries of events?

The present account attempts to combine personal memories of an epic struggle fifty and more years ago with all the broader contemporary documents that have subsequently become available. The main pleasure in researching the naval history of those years has been that, often, what has been an unrecorded memory is now discovered in greater detail in the official reports. What follows could not have been done without the many other writings in the intervening years, but my main source has been the Public Record Office at Kew.

What is different, and perhaps unpalatable, is the 'warts and all' approach. One hopes that, by the 1990s, no sensitivities can have survived to be trampled upon; but can we really understand the past if some aspects of it are permanently dissembled? An anti-heroic standpoint does, however, have its difficulties: how far can one go in the service of total truth? Should one indicate, for example, the supposed looters of survival rations from the ship's lifeboat? What has drinking at sea got to do with shipboard morale? Should the chaos caused to a ship's routine by a Senior Officer's inspection invoke only hilarity? The answer seems to lie in the comprehension such anecdotal examples may offer to wider problems.

This raw candour was not available to the classic post-war writers. Some of the memoirists were too close in time to risk giving offence; others were too lofty in authority to concern themselves with blemishes in the grand design. Only the impotent and disinterested participant-observer can bring such peccadilloes to light and only then perhaps at this decent interval in time. Nevertheless, despite the occasional individual weakness, one's own as well as that of others, it is possible to perceive that the fibre of the whole sub-society was more than strong enough to survive the test of battle.

[1] Allan Coles, 1993, *Invergordon Scapegoat*, Allan Sutton, p. 38.

CHAPTER 1

Introduction

The dockyard policeman on the main gate of Govan dock-yard west of Glasgow eyed my pristine brass buttons and the new wavy curl on the cuff of my doeskin uniform. It was June 1942 and the shortage of gold thread prevented my single stripe from entirely encircling my sleeve; the poverty of this meagre symbol of authority did nothing for my self-confidence.

'Yes?' he enquired, with calculated economy; he could tell a green 'un when he saw one.

'*HMS Narcissus*, please.' I said, importantly.

He nodded to what appeared to be an empty drydock about forty yards away.

'There she is, over there.'

The brevity of my nautical training had left me with two disabilities: on the one hand I was appallingly ignorant about many aspects of a sailor's life; on the other hand, bitter experience had taught me not to ask questions which might invite shaming laughter. When acting as the breach-worker, in a recently undergone gunnery course, I had innocently questioned the need to take my hand away from the breach-opening lever of a naval gun between discharges: 'Wouldn't it save time for me to hang on to the lever, Chief?' I asked brightly of the Gunner's Mate.

'Certainly, sir,' replied the gaitered dragon, after he had re-raised his jaw, 'so long as you did not mind being scraped off the bulkhead, where the gun's recoil would have sent you.'

1

So in Govan dockyard, instead of telling the dour guardian of the gate in my best Nelsonian manner that I saw no NARCISSUS, I peered again in the nodded direction. This time I could see the top of a mast protruding over the edge of the dockside. On closer inspection it transpired that my future home was undergoing a period of maintenance and repairs in a dry-dock intended for a much larger ship. As I looked down, along its 200 feet of length, I saw dock-yard workmen, dockyard 'mateys' as I would learn to call them, from stem to stern on the upper deck. They all wore cloth caps, whereas their foreman traditionally wore a bowler hat. From my high vantage-point I could see the black crown of the bowler hat progressing slowly around the deck; five yards in front of it the cloth caps were picking up their tools; five yards behind they were putting them down again.

At the bottom of the steep gangway which led from the dockside inboard, I found my very first comrade-in-arms: the boatswain's (bosun's) mate, conventionally dressed in a seaman's overcoat and cap and armed only with a bosun's call; this traditionally-shaped whistle was provided in the unlikely event that a ship's captain should wish to visit the ship in dockyard. Only in larger ships, of course, would the officer-of-the-day dance attendance on the gangway. With a crew of under a hundred men and only three watchkeeping officers, informality had imperceptibly become a dominant strategy; an informality which was reinforced by the ship being in dockyard hands. Not only were repairs and modifi-cations being carried out, but stores were being replenished and half the crew was away at home on hard-earned leave. So it was the bosun's mate who took me to the head of the wardroom ladder and I reported myself with as much ceremony as I could muster to the First Lieutenant.

Like a new boy at school, it was up to me to acquaint myself with my most immediate colleagues and then to widen my relationships eventually to all on board. The Captain was away on leave, which left the First Lieutenant in command. The latter was a relatively rare bird: he hailed from Hong Kong where he had served in the peacetime Royal Naval Volunteer Reserve. In wartime, the RNVR tended to be a catch-call category into which all naval officers were fitted if they were neither regular Royal Navy, nor professional ex-merchant navy and, therefore, Royal Naval Reserve. In the customarily British fashion, these distinctions had been seized upon to establish a mutually disparaging hierarchy of ability: RN officers were stereo-typed as gentlemen trying to be sailors; RNR were charac-terized as sailors trying to be gentlemen; and RNVR were stigmatized as neither, although they were at least attempt-ing to be both. Which role then, in the scale of skills, was implicitly regarded as the more important: for the purposes of leadership in battle, was it more desirable to be a gentle-man than a sailor?

The Officer Cadre

However, the RNVR canard could never be applied to Hugh Meeke, the First Lieutenant, and not just because of his apprenticeship in the peacetime RNVR: his job on board was to supervise the daily routine, in particular the discipline of the crew and their application to work. In all the time I was to know him, I hardly ever heard him raise his voice and the continuing tranquillity of the ship's life, even at times of great stress, was in no small measure due to his calm influence. At 35 he was one of the oldest men on board and certainly the oldest officer. Hugh Meeke's model impression upon my late teens always made it difficult for me to accept the frequent portrayals in British fictional drama, where the top man has often been represented as serene and just, forever curbing the brutal excesses of the second-in-command.

As I was to learn in NARCISSUS, an officer's principal obligation is to take prompt and informed decisions; thus there must always be an officer on the bridge of a ship at sea; he may be navigating, supervising the lookouts, conning the ship, taking emergency action in the temporary absence of the captain, or merely ensuring the maintenance of the ship's timetable. With four experienced watchkeepers apart from the captain, NARCISSUS could have maintained rotating watches: four hours on and twelve hours off. Standing watches were, however, the norm: the First Lieutenant stood from 8 to 12, a.m. and p.m., called the Forenoon and First watches; two officers stood the Morning and Dog watches, 4 to 8 a.m. and p.m.; and one officer stood the Middle and Afternoon watches, midnight to 4 a.m. and noon to 4 p.m.

This poor devil was cursed twice over; not only did he have the least popular watch, but he also had to take the new boy under his wing. It was my good fortune that he took on this duty with easy charm. Peter Gray was an actor and must have deeply resented being torn away from his vocation. His was also a sensitive soul, which had recoiled from the rough good humour and lack of privacy of the lower deck, to which he was of necessity subjected before he was commissioned. Without being a prude, he even found the occasionally lewd conversation of the wardroom mess more than he could stomach and would tend to retire to his cabin if he sensed that the subject was becoming tasteless. As my watchkeeping tutor, he was a willing teacher and what little I absorbed for the next two years was mainly down to him.

At the end of their period of home leave, the two remaining watchkeepers returned refreshed and, in their different ways, refreshing. Trevor Jones carried all the ebullience of his Celtic nature like a badge; irrepressibly extraverted he harried his equals and chivvied his subordinates with cheerful impartiality. He looked remarkably like a boyhood hero of mine, the great Welsh full-back Vivian Jenkins, whom I had seen, in his role as a schoolboy rugby coach, throw a ball half the width of a pitch. So in my eyes Trevor Jones could do no wrong.

To the tall dark Trevor the short blond Reg Edye was the Saxon antithesis. Reg was irrevocably uxorious, doting on his distant wife, outwardly mirthful, inwardly wishing it were all over so that he could get back to his cosy hearth. Of the five commissioned officers serving in HMS NARCISSUS when I arrived on board, Edye and Gray were married and the other three were bachelors.

Then there was the Captain. He was a remote figure. Somewhat Nordic in appearance, sardonic in mien, keeping himself to himself, delivering caustic and seemingly embittered comments on the developments of the day, he gave the impression of regretting the situation in which he found himself. No doubt professionally it must have seemed beyond a joke to have become involved with a load of bumbling amateur sailors in a savage life-and-death struggle. He certainly took his duties very seriously; whilst the ratings had their daily ration of rum at sea or in harbour, he and the other officers avoided alcohol at sea. This unwritten rule was always observed, apart from a single occasion, to which we can come later.

At the time of my arrival in June 1942, the Captain was aged 32, the First Lieutenant was 35 and the others were between 29 and 32; I was aged 19 and was the sole sub-lieutenant (at that age I should really have been a midshipman, but the Admiralty mistakenly thought it was recruiting a more mature 'Direct-entry Yachtsman'). The others were all full lieutenants; the Captain was pre-War RNR, betokening his Merchant Navy origins, and the rest were RNVR. In that peculiarly naval tradition of formalized respect for responsibility, irrespective of substantive rank, we watchkeepers called the First Lieutenant 'Sir'; we and he called the Captain 'Sir'. The Royal Navy had not changed much from the days of Cook and Bligh. No doubt that was one of its strengths; those strengths were going to be tested.

The Crew

It goes without saying that a ship's company during the Second World War would tend to be a microcosm of the society from which it was drawn: there was the privileged 'upper' class, represented by the officers in whom power and ultimate responsibility lay; there was the 'working' class, i.e. the ratings living in crowded and austere conditions on the Lower Deck; their toughness and invincible sense of humour would undoubtedly form the foundation of the Navy's eventual success.

I would learn that small-ship discipline was subtly different from that in cruisers and above; this would not be discernible immediately, because formalities of dress in harbour and interpersonal courtesies were as punctilious. Nevertheless, there seemed to be a tacit perception, between the ranks, of each other's problems: out on deck, at least, we all shared the same discomforts. I would soon discover, also, that remarks made in the heat of stress or battle, which in larger ships might have been construed as contrary to good order or worse, were usually greeted with a wry smile, as if contributing to the relaxation of tension.

In between those two classes there was the middle 'class' of petty officers; despite seeming withdrawn from the other two groups, these men were the true keepers of the soul of this nautical sub-society. Individuals of the other two may have misbehaved occasionally, but the petty officers never seemed to and their disapproval of the individual misdemeanour of those either above or below them could become fatal to a man's career, or even to a quiet life. The co-operation of the three classes remained the Navy's strength as long as the petty officers assented in the handling of the ship by the officers, and as long as the ratings feared their petty officers more than they feared the enemy. In spite of all the disasters to come, the proof of that contention lay in the outcome of the Battle.

The leader of that middle stratum of my new community was the Coxswain (henceforth Cox'n), who was also designated the Master-at-Arms; that is to say, he was the man who held the ship's wheel at action stations and who enforced the Captains discipline at other times. In NARCISSUS this pivotal post was held by a regular Royal Naval chief petty officer called Briggs; a suave character of saturine appearance whom nothing surprised or flustered.

The next most important petty officer, at least as far as the deck officers were concerned, was the Chief Bosun's Mate or, more familiarly, the 'Chief Buffer'. He supervised all working parties aboard the ship and, in that capacity, was the First Lieutenant's right-hand man. As befitted one who had to make the seaman work in often uncomfortable circumstances, if not by force of character then by physical presence, he was very large with a shock of red hair.

There was a chief engine room artificer, of course; but he and all his E.R.A.s and stokers belonged to a different tribe. The Chief E.R.A. dealt directly with the Captain until there was an engineer officer appointed eighteen months later. Most of the other specialist ratings were headed by leading seamen: so there was a leading signalman, a leading submarine detector, a leading sick berth attendant, a leading cook and so on. The leading rating I came first into contact with was, of course, Leading Officers' Steward Jim Neave, a charming and handsome man from King's Lynn, who mothered the inhabitants of the wardroom, although he was hardly any older than they were.

The bridge staff, i.e. officers, helmsmen, bos'n's mates (who were mainly there to see that their helmsman did not fall asleep and to raise the next watch on deck), signalmen, lookouts and the engine room staff, all worked watches at sea. The rest were so-called 'Daymen', turning to for work only after breakfast and spending all night in their bunks or hammocks; except that, at 'Action Stations', everyone had a waking role.

The Ship

HMS NARCISSUS was launched at Lewis's shipyard in Aberdeen on 29 April 1941 and displaced under a thousand tons. An original complement of 85 men rose in time to about a hundred and her main armament was one 4-inch mark IX breach-loading gun. She was designed to carry a minimum of 40 depth-charges filled with the explosive Amatol.

The role of all escort vessels was to ensure the safe arrival of food and war supplies, which were carried in a variety of merchant ships. Sloops, destroyers, frigates and corvettes were at sea to sink enemy submarines only insofar as this was the best way, in the long term, of completing the primary task of delivering convoys to their destinations. Driving and keeping a U-boat below the surface where, for the time being, it could do no damage was often the best alternative, given the frequent need to return to a thinly defended convoy.

Corvettes could be produced in the necessary numbers more cheaply and faster than any other escort vessel. They fulfilled the minimal requirements of a stable platform upon which to mount the means to find a submarine and to destroy it. In order to carry out this task this meant, at first, that a corvette should be equipped with an anti-submarine detector unit (called 'Asdic' throughout the RN, but 'Sonar' by the Americans), depth-charge throwers and rails and possess only sufficient sea-keeping endurance to enable it to escort coast-wise traffic. With the fall of France, however, U-boats could reach out from French bases in the Bay of Biscay into the Atlantic in search of their prey. This compelled the Admiralty to convert corvettes into ocean-going escorts. For this role they were supplied with Radio Direction Finders (R.D.F. now 'Radar'), an increased fuel capacity and an extended forecastle; this latter modification had the dual advantage of enabling them to cope with heavier Atlantic seas and of housing the larger crews needed. The normal gunnery equipment of a 4-inch breach-loading cannon, an anti-aircraft quick-firing 2-pounder and two 20 mm Oerlikons was unaffected. During the ship's annual refit in 1942, a forward throwing anti-submarine weapon, the 'Hedgehog', was installed to overcome tactical problems with the rearward-firing depth-charges. So this was the standard to which NARCISSUS had been modified by the time I joined her in June 1942.

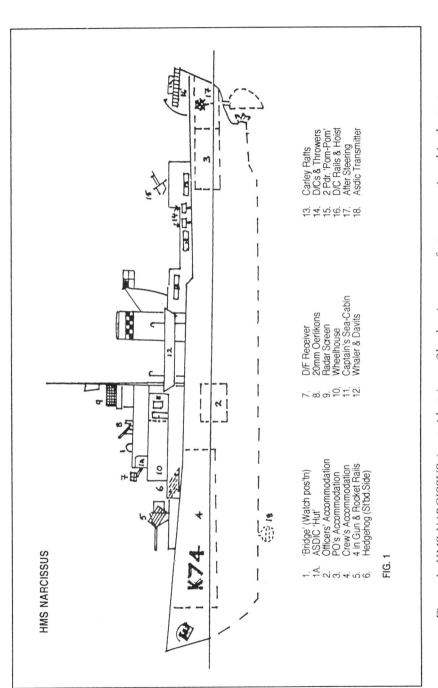

HMS NARCISSUS

K74   FIG. 1

1.   'Bridge' (Watch pos'tn)
1A. ASDIC 'Hut'
2.   Officers' Accommodation
3.   PO's Accommodation
4.   Crew's Accommodation
5.   4 in Gun & Rocket Rails
6.   Hedgehog (St'bd.Side)

7.   D/F Receiver
8.   20mm Oerlikons
9.   Radar Screen
10. Wheelhouse
11. Captain's Sea-Cabin
12. Whaler & Davits

13. Carley Rafts
14. D/Cs & Throwers
15. 2 Pdr. 'Pom-Pom'
16. D/C Rails & Hoist
17. After Steering
18. Asdic Transmitter

Figure 1: HMS NARCISSUS (port side to); profile showing some features mentioned in the text.

The original and very detailed Admiralty designs for the Modified Flower-class Corvette have recently been published (see Reference 1 for this chapter), but, even though authoritative, they cannot give comprehensive particulars for every vessel: individual ships adapted designated spaces to their special needs or, on the other hand, acquired equipment in response to operational experience. So, for the sake of the particular history of NARCISSUS, a simple line-drawing is offered here which leaves out many commonplace features, such as rigging, aerials, lockers, ventilators, etc., but includes at least two features which are underplayed or absent from more elaborate publications (see Figure 1).

For example, a space within the bridge superstructure is commonly shown as 'settee'. One may reasonably ask: for what purpose was a settee provided behind the wheelhouse of a warship? There seems to be no good reason why its purpose in NARCISSUS should not be the one intended: namely, to serve as the Captain's night-cabin. From there he could reach the side of the officer-of-the-watch in a couple of bounds, if he heard any alarm or unusual sound or movement. Similarly, there is no indication in recent publications of an important modification made to the night-time fighting capacity of escort vessels late in 1943: the fitting of illuminating-rocket rails on either side of the main armament shield. Had these been fitted before September 1943, the outcome of NARCISSUS's head-to-head encounter then with U-270 might have been different.

Churchill's 'Flowers of the Ocean'

The apparent paradox of giving the names of land-flowers to war-ships (sic) merely follows a long tradition. Our NARCISSUS, for example, was the tenth ship of her name to be commissioned into the Royal Navy. The first was a frigate which gave a rather inauspicious start to the name, during Popham's 'adventure' in the River Plate[2]; the antepenultimate was a sloop in Beatty's day. The most 'Glorious' of all, in date as well as in fate, was our immediate predecessor, a yacht of 816 tons, armed with two 2-pounder guns: she was sunk off Dunkirk by aircraft attack on the last full day of the evacuation of the British Expeditionary Force, the First of June 1940.

The task of naming ships would not have been a mere sinecure for a committee of civil servants. Proper consideration would have had to be taken of historical precedent: one imagines that there is an absolute bar in the Royal Navy to naming any naval ship after Captain Bligh's notorious ship. Disastrous sinkings, on the other hand, do not seem to proscribe the inheritance of a name unless, of course, there was some shameful connotation: to be lost with all hands seems to be alright in this context, as long as it was in the process of 'engaging the enemy more closely', in the immortal phrase. Some support for this latter thesis is offered by the existence today of an HMS ITCHEN, the immensely tragic fate of whose predecessor will be described later.

One did wonder if awarding the name 'Narcissus' to a ship ever gave the Admiralty's naming committee pause for thought. Jolly Jack, after all, is encouraged quite rightly to identify with his ship. Would some seaman with a penchant for the Classics ever ask a member of her crew if he spent his time hanging over the side admiring himself in the water? To Their Lordships' representatives apparently, the risk of embarrassment seemed to be negligible.

One flower name that certainly did slip under their guard, however, was 'Pansy'. HMS PANSY was duly incorporated as a corvette into the Flower Class. Too late the Admiralty hastened to have it changed to HMS HEARTSEASE, which appears in dictionaries as 'a common name for the pansy . . . an infusion of which was once through to ease the love-sick heart'. One can just imagine what, in a dockside tavern, a hairy-chested stoker from another ship would have made of that one. In early 1942, when the United States were caught short of convoy escort vessels, 'Lend-Lease' in reverse got Their Lordships off the hook: one corvette turned over to them was HEARTSEASE. One would like to think that the American re-naming committee had a sense of humour as well as a desire for continuity, for our corvette then became USS COURAGE![3]

North Atlantic convoy escorting organization

This was the especial concern of the Western Approaches Command of the Royal Navy and initially comprehended three escort forces working out Liverpool on the Mersey, Londonderry in Northern Ireland and Greenock on the Clyde. Each Force had a variable number of escort groups under command, usually two regular and other additional ones, which latter could either be given special tasks or could be used as replacements for the regular groups. With the new need to sustain the Russians through the Arctic and to replace the American withdrawals towards the Pacific by the beginning of 1942, five regular groups were allocated to the three Western Approaches' bases by February 1942, each comprising an 'H' class destroyer and five to six corvettes. The five destroyers were the survivors of the so-called 'Requisitioned Brazilian' H-class of 1940, HURRICANE (B1), HESPERUS (B2), HARVESTER (B3), HIGHLANDER (B4), and HAVELOCK (B5); the corvettes were all from the Flower class. By September 1943 two further regular groups, B6 and B7, had been added, one each to the Liverpool and Londonderry Forces. B3 remained as the single group in Clyde Escort Force.

B3 Escort Group

'B' groups were mainly British in content ('British' embracing all those European crews who either brought their own ship with them, like the Poles, or were allocated ships, like the Norwegians). 'C' groups denoted Canadians, whose

Navy experienced the greatest expansion of any during the war years. Despite containing an unusually high number of Allies, specifically Polish and French, B3 remained a British group. It might be thought that language, cultural and personality differences would lead to misunderstandings and chaos in action. In the event, this may only ever have occurred once in B3 Group in the face of the enemy, as far as I am aware. Credit for this unity of purpose must be given to the Naval Liaison staffs which accompanied each Allied ship's company, comprising an officer, signals and coding ratings and a submarine-detection cadre.

Cynics averred that the main function of these was 'to keep an eye on what our Allies were doing', but there was a very real problem as to how to interpret and follow the Senior Officer of the Group's intentions. Most of the Allied ships' captains spoke excellent English (indeed some of them married British wives) and I believe that any small disagreement was probably intentional and brought into play a Nelsonian blind eye. Some credit must also go to the Senior Officers chosen to lead the Group. Both the leaders I knew seemed to understand and sympathize with the special difficulties of their allies and seemed to generate, respectively, affection and co-operation in return.

So B3 Group contained, at various times, two to four destroyers, including one to three Polish units, plus the occasional frigate and a trawler and/or rescue ship from time to time. The destroyers, essential for the offensive capacity of convoys by virtue of their speed, which could overtake a surfaced U-boat, were led by HMS HARVESTER until March 1943; she had a complement of 145 men. The three Polish destroyers comprised ORP BURZA, an original escaper from the Baltic in the first days of 1939, with a complement of 155 men; ORP GARLAND, an ex-British G-class, loaned to the Polish Navy for the duration of the War; and ORP PIORUN, similarly an ex-British N-class destroyer.

The most permanent element, however, always involved the corvettes: four or five of them was the norm, allowing for time off for refits, out of a regular membership of six;

two of them were British and four Free French. Thirty Flower-class corvettes would be lost during the War, fourteen of them due to U-boat torpedoes.

The territorial identities represented by such titles as 'Clyde' or 'Newfoundland' Escort Force faded as group membership stabilized and as the groups plied more broadly, but they lived on in insignia: the ships of B3 carried a, probably faded, blue and yellow chequered band around the tops of their funnels until the end. In the 1940s these insignia, in black and white, were worn around the caps of only Scottish policemen, so I vaguely supposed our funnel bands were a reference to being based in Scotland. Not a bit of it. Over 50 years later I find that they were the inspiration of the first leader of B3 Group, Commander A. J. Baker-Cresswell, in BULLDOG: blue and yellow squares were of course the pattern of a naval flag signifying the number '3'![4] Commander Baker-Cresswell is also credited with selecting the rather fetching livery, or camouflage colours, in which the ships were clothed for the North Atlantic: pale mauve and white.[5]

Although the Group's Senior Officer, a three-ringed Commander, was like God at sea in his omnipotence, with the power to decline the advice of even the Admiralty though politely, administratively he answered to the Post-Captain (four rings) of Destroyers (Captain 'D') ashore in Greenock. So that this potentate should, presumably, not feel beached by being on shore, Captain 'D' Greenock's headquarters were designated as His Majesty's Ship ORLANDO; such shore establishments were commonly known as 'stone frigates'. Captain 'D', Greenock, in his turn, deferred to an even greater nabob, the Flag Officer, Glasgow, whose stone frigate was HMS SPARTIATE.

The Convoys

The first and last purpose of escort groups was to ensure the safe arrival of the merchant ships which constituted the lifeline for Britain, bringing most of the food for survival and much of the munitions needed for eventual victory. In any writing on the Battle of the Atlantic it is now almost obligatory to refer to Churchill's famous dictum that the only thing that ever really frightened him during the War was the U-boat peril.

It was undoubtedly the memory of the doom-laden months of February and March of 1917, when merchant shipping losses mounted during the First World War, which kept him aware of the danger in the Second. However many land- and air-victories were achieved in the course of both conflicts, it was only the Navy which could lose the war in an afternoon. In the Second War this axiom would refer not to the German High Seas Fleet, but only to the wolf-packs of U-boats. The consequences of failure to curb their predations would be disastrous.

Scoffers often attempt to pillory military leaders for fighting the battles of the previous war all over again. Yet one battle which had to be fought again, even in the same basic style, was the convoy battle. Despite the addiction of some admirals to patrolling the sea-lanes as an effective antidote to undersea warfare, the system of closely escorting merchant ships was immediately put into practice by the Royal Navy, insofar as the resources allowed. Fast, often passenger, ships were allowed to travel independently, as were those freighters which were considered to be out of the cruising range of U-boats; and many paid the penalty for doing so. In the highly vulnerable waters of the North Atlantic, however, merchant ships were collected in the estuaries of, for example, the Mersey and the Clyde into groups of up to 40 or 50 and despatched together westwards under the care of a naval escort. Likewise, the harbours of Halifax and New York on the North American side of the ocean saw convoys collected and delivered in the same way (see Figure 2).

The Shape of Convoys

Experience in the First War had shown that massed shipping, on an ocean crossing, could be protected better when spread over a broad front than in two or three long lines. In the Second World War a typical convoy of, say, 44 ships would be allocated positions in columns on a grid whose corner co-ordinates would be 11, 111, 114 and 14 (reading in a clockwise direction from the left front, i.e. port-wing, corner; see the diagram below).

The distance to be maintained between columns was generally 1000 yards and the distance between ships in a column was intended to be 800 yards, but this might vary according to circumstances. This would give a reasonably manageable frontage of about five sea-miles. Later on in the War convoys needed to be spread over up to 22 columns; convoy SL147/MKS38 was an example of this great width, having a frontage of 11 miles. When it is considered that the distance to the horizon at sea level was only eight miles, the implications can be imagined.

Allocation would not be haphazard: 'portions' of convoy with a common destination would be allocated places in the convoy appropriate to their direction of travel from the 'Split Position' on the further side of the Atlantic Ocean. For example, an eastwards convoy might be so arranged that ships due to split off after reaching 7° to 10° West would have ships for Loch Ewe in the port-wing columns, ships for the Clyde on the port side of centre, ships for the Mersey on the starboard side of centre and ships for Milford Haven in the starboard-wing columns.

Within these portions, consideration would also be given to the value and urgency of the cargo of each ship; human life being of the highest value, then oil for fuelling and ammunition for keeping up the fight. Food, wood and iron-ore seem not to have been given high priority, and often featured on the exposed wings.

The leading ships of the sixth, ninth and third columns would carry the convoy commodore, vice-commodore and rear-commodore respectively. In Navy fashion each was recognizable by his flag, flown at the masthead: a broad white burgee with a blue cross identifying a commodore, Royal Naval Reserve; a red burgee for his vice-commodore; and a white pennant with a horizontal black stripe for the rear-commodore. Sometimes the positions in the convoy of vice- and rear-commodore's ships were dropped back to give depth and certainty to the succession to command; which was a wise precaution in view of the fact that no fewer than twenty-one convoy commodores perished with their ships. The commodore's ship would have been selected partly on account of the height of its mainmast and therefore the visibility of its signalling equipment. It was also only natural that a certain level of comfort was necessary for the solace of these aged stalwarts: unheated accommodation and a bridge unduly exposed to the weather would undermine the dynamism of, and might soon snuff out, a sixty-year old commodore.

There would also be a whole hierarchy of ships designated as 'signal repeaters' (for such crucial orders as emergency turns away from submarine threat) both by light and by siren: thus in a convoy grid, numbers 32 and 102 might be designated light repeaters and sound repeaters would include not only the column leaders but also numbers 33, 53, 73, 93. Even so, sleepy watchkeepers might miss an emergency turn at night, steam on and find themselves along in the ocean next morning!

The convoy commodore was normally a retired admiral or master seaman, recalled to an occupation where crustiness was a positive asset, and serving in the rank of 'Commodore RNR'. Woe betide the freighter which made too much smoke or straggled unduly; not only would the commodore put in an adverse written report, but he was likely to speak roughly to the offender at the time by whatever means were available. Commodores were also not above reporting on the performance of the escorting warships, but usually in a congratulatory fashion.

Within the convoy there were likely to be oilers to top up

Table 1.

11 Army Passgrs Genrl.	21 Genrl. Sugar	31 Explosives	41 Army Pass. Gen.	51 Army Pass.	61 Army Pass. Steel	71 Navy Stores	81 Gen.	91 Kerosene Gen.	101 Gen.	111 (Few) Passgrs
12 Sugar	22 Aviation Gas	32 Genl.	42 Luboil D/Chgs	52 Luboil D/Chgs	62 –	72 Depth Chgs.	82 High Octane	92 High Oct.	102 High Oct.	112 Genl.
13 Sugar	23 Lub/oil	33 Planes Gas	43 Pass. Expls.	53 High Octane	63 –	73 Gas	83 Gas	93 Gas Expls.	103 Expls.	113 Expls.
14 –	24 –	34 Expls.	44 Expls.	54 High	64 –	74 Expls.	84 Expls.	94 Expls.	104 –	114 –

any escort vessels which might be running low and some ships would carry nets, which they would stream as a protection against torpedo attack, but these would tend to slow them down and cause them to straggle. The average speed of fast convoy (ON westward-bound, HX eastward-bound) was nine knots and that of a slow convoy (ONS westward, SC eastward) was seven knots; from the meeting point with the ocean escort to the dispersal point on the opposite side of the ocean might take 8 days with a fast convoy and twelve with a slow; but these might be extended by adverse weather conditions.

Thus a specimen convoy, with the freight carried by each ship (actually HX 259, October '43):

In Table 1, 'Gen.' stands for General Stores, 'Pass.' stands for Passengers, 'High Oct.' stands for Petrol, 'D/Chgs.' stands for Depth Charges, 'Expls.' stands for Explosives and 'Luboil' stands for Lubricating Oil; additional General cargoes are recorded as being carried all over the convoy and are here excluded.

References

[1] D. K. Brown, 1996, *The Design and Construction of British Warships, 1939–1945* Conway, Volume II, page 50; also see J. McKay & J. Harland, 1993, *The Flower Class Corvette AGASSIZ* in the Anatomy of the Ship series, Conway, p. 150.

[2] John D. Grainger, 1995, 'The Navy in the River Plate, 1806–1808', *The Mariner's Mirror*, Vol. 81, p. 293.

[3] *All the World's Fighting Ships, 1922–1946*, Conway, 1980, p. 62.

[4] David Kahn, 1991, *Seizing the Enigma*, Souvenir Press, p. 7.

[5] A photograph of BULLDOG towing U-110, in Baker-Cresswell's obituary at the age of 96 in the Daily Telegraph on 7 March 1997, shows her wearing the chequered band inherited by B3 Group.

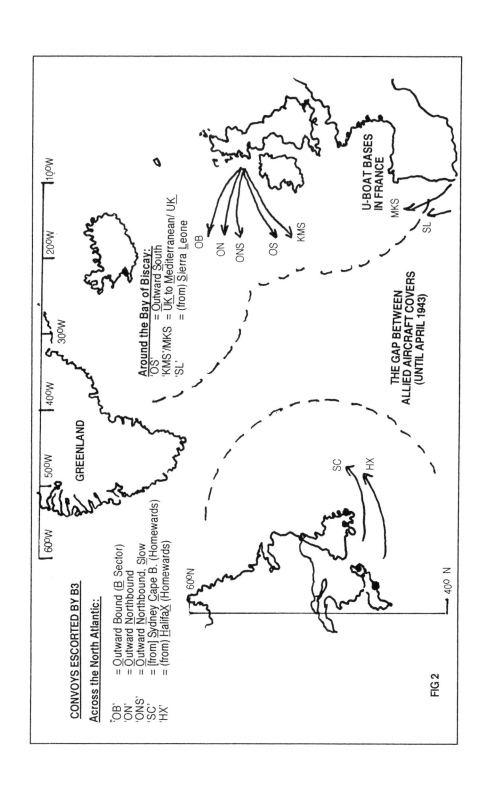

CONVOYS ESCORTED BY B3

Across the North Atlantic:

'OB' = Outward Bound (B Sector)
'ON' = Outward Northbound
'ONS' = Outward Northbound, Slow
'SC' = [from] Sydney Cape B. (Homewards)
'HX' = (from) Halifax (Homewards)

Around the Bay of Biscay:
'OS' = Outward South
'KMS'/MKS = UK to Mediterranean/ UK
'SL' = (from) Sierra Leone

U-BOAT BASES
IN FRANCE

THE GAP BETWEEN
ALLIED AIRCRAFT COVERS
(UNTIL APRIL 1943)

GREENLAND

FIG 2

CHAPTER 2

Brothers-in-Arms

Confidence to confront the daily threats from Nature and the human enemy in the North Atlantic was greatly enhanced by the knowledge that one was not facing those perils alone. There were shipmates and allies who were close at hand and visible and there were friends and backers who were more remote but who could be relied upon for help.

Perhaps for NARCISSUS, which was based upon the Clyde and never in all the two years I was with her went near the Mersey, Western Approaches Command in Liverpool seemed the most remote backers. It has only been long after the War, when the full details have emerged of the Ultra secret, that the directing roles of strategic commanders have been appreciated properly, at least by 'foot soldiers' in the Battle such as I. Now we can all recognize the vital work done by the Submarine Tracking Room in the Admiralty and by the Western Approaches Tactical Unit. From them came the information to senior officers of escort groups about U-boat concentrations; also from them came the evolving tactics that were to win the Battle eventually. To the minor players in ships at sea B3 Escort Group had often seemed to be on its own.

As for administrative, but equally elevated, naval officers ashore like Captain (D) Greenock and Flag Officer Glasgow, the sailors' awe was properly tempered by the sort of jocularity appropriate to a dangerous fish out of water. There was, for example, the favourite anecdote, possibly apocryphal but told with every assurance of veracity, about our Glasgow Admiral. It seems that on one winter's evening he was alone in the back of his staff car being driven from Glasgow towards Greenock. On a stretch of country road his Wren driver pulled into the side and, blushing, jumped out to attend to a small personal need. Afterwards she drove the remaining dozen or so miles quickly, to make up for the lost time. Despite the lateness of the hour, the naval guard was turned out for the great man at his destination. The Wren who, out of embarrassment, had neither looked behind nor spoken since the stop, swung open the rear door. The Admiral had evidently attended to his own small need as well, for he was not there.

The Women's Royal Naval Service

The Wrens of the Royal Navy performed two functions, one manifest and the other latent. They contributed, of course, shore-side tasks like training, stewarding, victualling, boat-handling and armament maintenance, upon which an efficient fleet depended. In these roles they freed their male counterparts for combat at sea.

Their pervasive presence in harbour, however, exerted a civilizing influence upon men who might otherwise have become brutalized by the harshness of their work. Leisure time in harbour and on periodic leave away from the port was often spent with the Wrens met by sailors in the course of their service; indeed, after the War many would marry them.

The number of Wrens in Greenock, where NARCISSUS was based, was not large but always inspiring. One of their officers remains in my mind for purely idiosyncratic reasons: because of my relatively rare surname, I had developed an 'ugly duckling' complex; I had never met another 'Coy' and wished I had. One day alongside in Gourock in 1943 a Third Officer, WRNS, came on board NARCISSUS and I was introduced. 'How interesting,' said this attractive woman 'I am engaged to a Coy.' It is with vicarious pleasure that I read in the press, on 27th April 1996, that (Lt. Cdr. RN Rtd.) Geoffrey Coy and Barbara Stewart are celebrating their golden wedding anniversary.

Brothers-in-the-air

The Royal Air Forces of Britain and Canada, flying Wellingtons, Whitleys, Sunderlands and Catalinas from shore bases in Britain and Newfoundland could reach out only 600 miles westwards, 200 miles eastwards into the North Atlantic and only 500 miles southwards of Iceland, by the end of 1942. The gap in the middle could only be covered by a few very-long-range Liberator aircraft.

In the middle portion of a crossing of the Atlantic the airmen were thus able to interact with convoys for only a very short while at the extremity of their operating range. It was in this vulnerable area, of course, that U-boats congregated and, once or twice, our aircraft could be seen to be machine-gunning what had to be a shadowing, sur-faced U-boat.

Recognition signals exchanged with Allied aircraft were heartening human contacts in an otherwise hostile environment. Such signals were also, of course, necessary checks upon the identity and intentions of any aerial intruder: a solitary plane in the eastern Atlantic area circling the horizon was sometimes found to be a German sent out to find the convoy for a nearby U-boat pack. Another favourite story had it that an irritable escort commander signalled to such a plane: 'Go round the other way! You are making me dizzy!'; to which the German pilot amiably replied 'Certainly'; and did.

American and Russians

Equally remote were Britain's numerically major allies, the Americans and the Russians, both no doubt deeply preoccupied with what they had to consider to be the more essential life-or-death struggles in the Pacific and the Eastern land-front respectively. The only American fighting ships I was to see in the North Atlantic from mid-1942 to mid-1944 was the escort carrier USS BOGUE with its two escorting destroyers. From the 1st March 1943 this token unit replaced all US escort vessels, which were henceforth withdrawn from the North Atlantic and concentrated further south, on the routes between the Americas and the Mediterranean.[1]

The only Russian that I encountered in the North Atlantic was one affable naval officer from a visiting minesweeper, at a Canadian wardroom party. The Battle of the North Atlantic was thus primarily a British and Canadian affair, gallantly and ably assisted by the European naval survivors of the German tidal wave which swept eastwards in 1939 and westwards in 1940. There had been developed, however, a massive American naval base at Argentia, in Placentia Bay, Newfoundland. For B3 Group this became the normal western terminus for ocean escort groups; repairs could be carried out under the aegis of a large American depot ship in the base, the USS PRAIRIE, and some recreation could be enjoyed there by the British crews, although no leave away from the ships was granted. This base at Argentia was one of many which the Americans were permitted to establish on what was then British colonial soil in the western hemisphere, in return for the fifty over-age destroyers transferred to British and Canadian flags.

The confused sovereignty of this situation was brought home on my very first visit to the American naval base: three of us had enjoyed an evening ashore and were strolling back to the corvette in what we had thought to be merely a nonchalant manner, when out of the shadow of dockside warehouse came a clear twang: 'There goes a bunch of goddam Limeys; walking like they own the place!' The rational response should have been for us to turn aside and explain as calmly and as earnestly as possible that, – well – yes as a matter of fact we did 'own the place' and that, like any respectable freeholder, having given warning of a visit, we had every right and duty of inspection to see that the leaseholders were treating it properly. The 'gobs' in the shadows had evidently failed to achieve a traditional rumble in the canteen and had high hopes of this chance encounter. We, even in our slightly inebriated and insouciant condition, could recognize the invitation for what it was and that further debate would not be a good idea. So, rather regretfully, we chose the better part of valour and moved discreetly on.

On the face of it, the Americans seemed to have done best out of that deal in 1940: they had obtained access to an arc of east-facing harbours which would protect them from an on-rushing Germany intent upon world domination; Great Britain, on the other hand, had surrendered the leasehold in exchange for a group of old vessels first launched at the end of the first World War; fewer than half of these fifty destroyers would still be serving by the end of 1942.[2]

Winston Churchill, however, was in no doubt about the latent function of the exchange. Whereas it was presented to the American people as a means whereby, in the then likelihood of the successful invasion of the British Isles, the British fleet might be kept out of Hitler's hands by attracting it across the Atlantic, the real effect of the deal was to bind the United States to the Allied cause. Even if this 'unneutral' act did not immediately persuade the Germans to declare war on the United States, its significance would be lost on no-one because, in Churchill's own words, 'It marked the passage of the United States from being neutral to being non-belligerent.'[3]

In this transaction without losers there was one more group of winners. The US Navy would provide the hundreds of technical staff needed to operate this bleak naval base of Argentia, but other workers would be required for more mundane tasks: for example, sixty local women were recruited for the base's laundry. By the time I first saw Argentia, these stalwarts had been the sole consolation for hundreds of lonely Americans, for many months on the frozen tundra of southern Newfoundland. They were the belles of the Armed Services' clubs in Argentia. After work in the laundry not a night needed to pass without a date with an admiral, or a post-captain at least; mere commanders could hardly get a look-in. It is, perhaps, uncharitable to wonder how these ladies managed to reconcile themselves to outback Newfoundland once they had tasted Argentia. In today's climate they would undoubtedly be offered counselling and even compensation for the shock. In September 1994 America finally closed her naval base at Argentia, which at its peak had housed up to 20,000 soldiers, sailors and civilians.

'Newfies' and Canadians

An alternative western terminus to Argentia on the North Atlantic convoy run for B3 Group was the capital of Newfoundland: St John's. This former fishing village lay in an enclosed inlet and could be approached only through a fissure in that huge escarpment which forms the eastern seaboard of Newfoundland. The town itself seemed to be constructed entirely of wood and had an old-world charm which, naturally, was quite absent from Argentia.

It was also more excitingly populated by both sexes: the girls in the shops were prettier than those we had been allowed to observe in Argentia. More European-type forms of recreation seemed to be possible in St John's – games of rugby on the frozen tundra were a painful option – but undoubtedly the main centre of attraction was the social club. It was here that serious drinking could be undertaken. Access to the club was via a spiral staircase up the side of a wooden building and, inevitably, it was called 'The Crow's Nest'; rather more perversely, we knew it as 'The Buzzard's Crutch'.

Here we would meet what turned out to be our principal partners in the North Atlantic enterprise, the Royal Canadian Navy. The Canadians had always provided most of the escort ships for the local convoys on the western side of the Atlantic. Loaded freighters and tankers would assemble in such harbours as New York or Halifax, Nova Scotia, and be brought in company to the Western Ocean Meeting Point, usually southeast of Placentia Bay in Newfoundland, where we or some other ocean escort group would conduct forty or more merchant ships in broad phalanxes to their British destinations.

The years 1940 and 1941 had been hard and difficult for North Atlantic escort vessels: bereft by the defeat of our major ally, France, the Royal Navy had to face a nearby, but widely spread, enemy coastline with insufficient ships and inadequate equipment for the changed convoying task. In consequence Britain suffered mounting losses in those opening two years.

By 1942, however, new warship-building, modifications (especially the lengthening of corvette hulls to accommodate the Atlantic swell) and better electronic detection gear had begun to rectify the balance of forces. Now new areas of conflict started to dilute the concentration of naval resources once again: the threat of invasion to Malta had to be countered by escorting reinforcements and supplies to the Mediterranean; in order to keep the Russians from collapsing, or worse, convoys of supplies had to run the gauntlet of dive-bombers and U-boats off the Norwegian coast to Murmansk; something had to be done about the coming carnage on the American east coast consequent upon the United States being drawn into the War by Japan.

So 1942 saw escort groups diminished. Nevertheless, hope was buoyed up by the rumour that dozens of corvettes and frigates were abuilding in Canada on the Great Lakes and that, come the Spring and the thawing of the ice, they would all come sailing down the St Lawrence seaway to join in the Battle. The heavy building programme embarked upon by the Canadians was not, of course, matched by an equal reservoir of trained sailors. The regular pre-war Canadian Navy had been small; and professional fishermen were insufficient to man the volume of ships now coming on stream. In consequence, many of the new volunteers came from the prairie provinces and had, perhaps, never seen the sea before. They would, however, play a gallant and conspicuous role in 1943, especially in the March and September battles which were to prove so decisive against the U-boats.

The Free Polish Navy

An ally whose co-operation with B3 Group was even closer and whose keenness for battle was second to none was that remnant of the Polish Navy, which had escaped from the Baltic after the debacle of September 1940. The BURZA was the oldest, but still capable of 33 knots; launched by the French for a peacetime Poland in 1929, she was already on her way to the UK on the first of September 1939 (together with her consorts BLYSKAWICA and GROM). The GARLAND and PIORUN were younger, faster, British-built and transferred to the Polish flag in May and November 1940 respectively, i.e. long after Poland itself was overwhelmed. All three were manned by Polish volunteers and one or other of these destroyers regularly sailed with B3 Group. A British historian was to say that: 'Of all the navies of the United Nations, none has fought better under circumstances of extreme operational difficulty than the navy of Poland.'[4] It is therefore all the more extraordinary that a search of the library of the National Maritime Museum has failed to turn up a single history of the Polish contribution to the Battle of the Atlantic.

Whilst communication with them during the War was hindered by an opaque language barrier, the Poles left an indelible memory of panache and gaiety. The problems of domestic separation, however, tested even their brand of ingenuity: one of them confided in me that he had a puzzle to solve; how to tell his wife in England that his wife in Poland had escaped to the West! I had little doubt that they could charm birds out of the trees too, having seen two Poles neatly extract a couple of the famous laundry 'birds' from the middle of a hitherto happy tableful of Free Frenchmen in one of the Services' clubs at Argentia.

The Norwegians

Other allies also manned escort vessels in the Battle of the Atlantic: notably the Norwegians who received six corvettes, two of which were to be lost. The circumstances of one of these sinkings reminded us of the high qualities of Norwegian seamanship. The ship lost was the RNN MONTBRETIA and she had been torpedoed during the course of a long-drawn-out attack upon a submerged U-boat. The radio report of the sinking, received in NARCISSUS, went on to say that sixty Norwegian survivors had been picked up; which was greeted with general amazement. A torpedoed corvette normally went down in seconds. On this occasion that part of the crew which was not needed at the depth-charges, or at the guns, happened to be high above sea-level, watching for a tell-tale periscope whilst strung along the foremast. So that when the ship sank beneath them, the many lookouts just floated clear.

The Free French Navy

The closest allies in B3 Group were, of course, the Free French. Theirs was the bitterest preparation for the Battle: not only had their nation been defeated and thrust out of the War, but their main fleet had been given an ultimatum and then attacked by their erstwhile ally (us) at Mers-el-Kebir on 3 July 1940, with the loss of over a thousand French lives. On the same day French warships in British ports were seized in the face of, in two cases, armed resistance; one of the resisting crews was that of the giant submarine SURCOUF.[5]

In mid-1942 an ugly rumour was circulating among

British naval personnel that the large French submarine SURCOUF had been suspected of preying upon Allied, as opposed to Axis, shipping and that there had been no alternative to giving her a rendezvous with an American battleship, which proceeded to sink her. Leaving aside the improbability that a **battleship** would have been deemed the most suitable for this unpleasant task, the likelihood that the British officer and his communication ratings on board would also have been sacrificed in so cavalier a fashion caused the rumour to be discounted. Naturally, the rumour was never discussed with our French colleagues.

It was therefore surprising to see the story emerging again in the British press some forty years later. The loss of the SURCOUF had always been ascribed, in the reference books and in French naval accounts, to an accidental collision with an American merchant ship in the Caribbean.[6]

But once resurrected, the story would not go away, but the most convincing study of it was undertaken by an ex-submariner, Commander Richard Compton-Hall, who gave good reasons for rejecting the allegation that SURCOUF was a tragic renegade.[7] After the melancholy necessity of the British attack upon the French fleet at Mers-el-Kebir in 1940, the miracle was, not that so many proud Frenchmen subsequently threw in their lot with De Gaulle but, that any of them at all were prepared to ignore the injury they had just suffered at the hands of their erstwhile Allies. These brave and far-sighted men were steadily reinforced by fishermen who continued to slip quietly away from Breton and other fishing villages, unwilling to live under German rule.

Many of these 'rebels' were to man the nine Flower class corvettes which were transferred to the French flag. Four of these corvettes were regular members of B3 Group, based upon Greenock on the Clyde and today a memorial overlooking the town records their contribution and sacrifices.

A 'devil's advocate' would have to say at this point that the early attitude of the Free French to duty was considered to be mercurial: when the time came to leave harbour, go to sea and take up the escorting task, their alacrity and punctuality were scrutinized. Unfavourable comparisons were made with what today would be called the more 'gung-ho' posture of the Poles. Slighting remarks would be made about undue dalliance at the adjacent bar of the Bay Hotel in Gourock and references made to the domestic attractions of the ladies of Greenock.

To the slightly puritanical British middle-class of that era, the openly sexual liaisons, too, of the French of all classes were a matter for some astonishment, perhaps even for sublimated envy. No doubt it is, and for the French it was then, the most natural thing in the world to enliven an otherwise dour prospect with all the recreational pleasures that may be available. Even after this interval of over half a century, one of the most abiding memories, which one surviving British signalman retains from those days, is of taking the ship's signals log-book each morning when in harbour, to his French officer's hotel bedroom. There he would customarily hand over the night's signals across the recumbent form of an unembarrassed girl-friend.

In view of the rough treatment the French had suffered at our hands in 1940, I suppose the British might have been rather more indulgent towards our allies' cultural proclivities; but those were hard times, especially during the exhaustion and reverses of 1942. It may be that gaiety and a carefree attitude serve as antidotes to despair and pessimism; whereas, paradoxically, critical severity may well go hand-in-hand with an absolute optimism as to the eventual outcome.

Inter-allies attitudes changed, however. On March 11 1943 the Free French ship ACONIT sank two U-boats in the Atlantic within twelve hours, the only corvette to accomplish this feat. Thereafter, the first away from the dockside when the call came to proceed to sea was often the Free French. Guilt, rage, despair, loneliness, whatever it was that had suppressed their native enthusiasm was now purged and they took their rightfully honoured place in the Group.

It is an irony of history that ACONIT was the only survivor of a group of four Free French ships which, in 1941, had liberated the islands of St Pierre and Miquelon off the Canadian coast (on De Gaulle's orders and against the wishes of the American government); the other three ships were two corvettes, ALYSSE and MIMOSA, sunk by U-boats in 1942 and . . . SURCOUF.

One source of friction continued until the end, unfortunately: in their wisdom their Lordships of the Admiralty had decreed that certain tasks in a foreign ship under British command were to remain in British hands. The confidential books and communications were in the charge of a British Naval Liaison Officer (BNLO); he had a British staff of, usually, three signalmen, two coders and two radio operators.

Curiously it was not the insertion of these communications ratings which caused problems in FFS LOBELIA, but the appointment of a Higher Submarine Detector rating (HSD) which stimulated a minor mutiny among his French fellow-ratings. The captain of LOBELIA relates how, on the occasion of some Asdics shore training, three of his French Asdic operators refused to continue, complaining that at sea, whenever 'Action Stations' was sounded, i.e. in the presence of a real U-boat, the British HSD always took over control of the Asdic.[8]

De Morsier had to punish the ringleader and, thereafter, the two others who went ashore as a gesture of solidarity with their shipmate. The story not only illustrates the grievances of a subordinate ally but also highlights the difficulties faced by liaison staffs, who could hardly have been trained diplomatists and probably did not choose their situation in the first place. The BNLO would find himself in the situation, well-known in anthropology, of the Janus-figure: however much a village head-man may be devoted to the interests of his community, superior authorities may well regard him as their man and require him to impose their will. Similarly, the BNLO was not like a soviet commissar, but had to face both ways: as a member of the ship's company, the crew would rightly demand his loyalty to them; but the British Admiralty would also expect to be kept informed about what was going on in the ship.

The 'Fourth Service': the Merchant Navy

At first the concept of a 'participant in the Battle' embraced only those units which had clearly an active military role: so long as a ship had guns and reacted dynamically to an enemy presence, her crew of whatever nationality comprised 'comrades-in-arms'. As time passed, more and more ships developed an active capacity, sometimes a dual capacity. Freighters began to solve the problem of the gap in aircover over the mid-Atlantic by shipping a monster catapult on the forecastle; there were eventually 35 of these 'Catapult-Armed Merchant' (CAM) Ships. Their single Hurricane fighter aircraft could only be used once, as they had no facility to pluck it out of the sea when its fuel ran out. The extravagance of this method beggars belief, but was an indication of the desperation of the times and of the importance of the cargoes they were intended to protect. Although they had some successes, they were a stop-gap measure and 13 of these ships were lost.[9]

The next step was to have a 400/490-foot landing and take-off deck on a total of 19 bulk-carrying ships, 6 of which carried grain and 13 carried oil. These 'Merchant Aircraft Carrier' Ships (MAC) came into service in May 1943 with the SS EMPIRE MACALPINE. These were able to deploy up to four Swordfish aircraft on the open flight deck; servicemen manned the aircraft but the ships' crews were civilians.[10]

The logical outcome of this method of solving the mid-Atlantic problem was the purpose-built escort carrier with hangars and its own escorts. The North Atlantic would eventually get four support-carrier groups, two RN, one RCN and one USN.[11]

To the warship crews the merchant ships they escorted probably seemed the passive recipients of naval protection.

In the case of the ships of neutral countries no doubt this was so, but vessels of the combatant nations carried a sizable armament. A 4-inch gun at the stern would, for example require a crew of at least nine men; in the British case these guns were manned by 'Defensively Equipped Merchant Ship' (DEMS) personnel or Army gunners. American ships had a considerable 'Naval Guard' on board.

To those of us who were primarily concerned with anti-submarine warfare and operated, for the most part, out of the reach of German aircraft, it seemed a waste of manpower to arm freighters with 4-inch guns, which were ineffective against torpedoes or even against surface raiders. Nevertheless, the First Lord of the Admiralty calculated that 'not less than 100 independently-routed [i.e. not in convoy] merchantmen a year had been saved by the gunners and their equipment.'[12] Many DEMS gunners were awarded gallantry medals, no doubt mainly earned in an anti-aircraft role.

The Rescue Ships

These stretcher-bearers of the sea had an unenviable task. Their gallantry should certainly, one hopes, have been fully rewarded; and there is no doubt of their honourable place as brothers-in-arms. Whether or not they were actually armed, they were known to carry HF/DF sets which enabled them to locate U-boat signals and thus to contribute hugely to both the defensive and offensive powers of the warships. Stationed at the rear of the convoy, the rescue ship would not only be best placed to collect men and lifeboats from the water, but would also be ideally situated for the senior escort officer to combine its HF/DF bearing with his own and thus 'fix' a U-boat's position with some accuracy.

There were not many permanent rescue ships, so they must have been worked hard; and they suffered a high proportion of casualties. Out of the eleven purposely equipped to pluck seamen out of the sea and to care for their wounds, no fewer than four were lost; two of these losses occurred in the notorious first months of 1943.[13]

So, apart from the Canadians and the Merchant Navy, Allied contributions to the Battle were few in number, but enormous and uplifting in respect of morale; their presence was a constant reminder that there was more at stake in this Battle than just our own personal survival.

References

[1] Correlli Barnett, 1991, *Engage the Enemy More Closely*, Hodder & Stoughton, p. 481.

[2] *Ibid.*, pp. 596–7.

[3] Winston Churchill, 1985, *The Second World War*, Vol. II, pp. 357–8.

[4] Brian Tunstall, quoted in *All the World's Fighting Ships*, 1922–1946, Conway Maritime Press, 1980, p. 348.

[5] The French submarine was named after a famous Breton privateer who preyed upon English shipping at the end of the eighteenth century; his statue can be seen on the walls of St Malo, with his finger still pointing towards Plymouth.

[6] E.g. P. de Morsier, 1972, *Les Corvettes de la France Libre*, France Empire.

[7] Richard Compton-Hall, 1985, *Submarine Warfare: The Monsters and the Midgets*, Blandford Press, p. 50 et seq.

[8] de Morsier, *op. cit.*, pp. 90–1.

[9] John Slader, 1994, *The Fourth Service. Merchantmen at War, 1939–1945*, Rober Hale, pp. 301–2.

[10] *Ibid.*, p. 303.

[11] Barnett, *op. cit.*, p. 584.

[12] Slader, *op. cit.*, p. 50.

[13] *Ibid.*, p. 145.

*Royal Naval College Greenwich, where Direct Entry Reserve Officers
were inducted in 1942.*

Induction Course of March 1942, including 7 RNR and 9 RANVR. The director was Commander MacLean RNR (seated 6th from the left) who later became Commodore of Cunard Line.

German Enigma Coding machine, similar to the one 'rescued' from U-110 by BULLDOG.

CHAPTER 3

The Clyde Escort Force acquires NARCISSUS

In May 1941 NARCISSUS was still only a gleam in the eye of her distinguished foster parents-to-be. These were two convoy escort groups based upon the Clyde, 3EG and 4EG, which would eventually coalesce into the British 3rd Escort Group (B3). An opportunity would fall to the leader of 3EG to provide his country with a service which every naval or military commander dreams of: an insight into the mind of the enemy.

On 9th May 1941 3EG was escorting convoy OB318 south of Iceland when it was attacked by several U-boats. The corvette AUBRETIA managed to depth-charge U-110 to the surface and the submarine was then abandoned. When the destroyer BULLDOG arrived, Commander A. J. Baker-Cresswell RN sent Sub-Lieutenant D. E. Balme RN across to the wallowing U-boat to salvage what he could. The U-boat captain, apparently realizing that his code-books had not been ditched, swam back and, as he was clambering up the side of the German vessel, was shot dead by the sea-boat's crew; this detail does not appear in any of the Admiralty records I have read, but is reported by two subsequent authors.

An historian, Ronald Lewin, puts Lemp's fate rather more tentatively and diplomatically: my interpretation of this apparent disparity between writers is that, perhaps, Lemp did commit what was tantamount to 'suicide' when he realized that he had left his Enigma aboard. Any doubts about the morality of this deed are assuaged by the identification of the Captain of U-110 as Fritz Julius Lemp who, in U-30, had sunk the passenger liner ATHENIA on the first evening of the war.

Subsequently Balme extracted, at some huge risk to himself and to his sea-boat's crew, a whole Enigma ciphering machine, key tables for officer grade messages, procedures for enciphering, the system for changing settings and the U-boat Short Signal Book.[1] One might ask what had inspired the Captain of BULLDOG to make this deeply influential capture? An historian of the Enigma saga ascribes it to Baker-Cresswell's recollection of a similar coup during the First World War, when Russians salvaged code books from the German cruiser MAGDEBURG. The Admiralty had certainly been showing interest already in the internal layout of U-boats, as is shown by an article in its Monthly Submarine Report for January 1941 ('What happens inside a U-boat').[2] In April 1940 the Royal Navy had 'luckily' captured settings for the Engima machine from the German patrol boat VP2623 off Narvik[3]; this and other *human* intelligence windfalls (gathered initially by a Polish organization) had excited the aspirations of *signal* intelligence. The subsequent vagueness of the records about convoy OB318 also suggest a nail-biting recognition of what Balme had achieved. All they say about this potentially Battle-winning event is 'BULLDOG opened fire with the 4.7 inch . . . the U-boat eventually sank'; and 'AUBRETIA . . . damaged the U-boat . . . and forced her to surface at 1235. U-110 was immediately abandoned and subsequently sank.'[4] The words 'eventually' and 'subsequently' represent a tortured triumph of necessary dissimulation over the complete truth.

The Admiralty was, of course, very grateful to the three leading players: by 1944 Baker-Cresswell was Chief Staff Officer (Operations) of Western Approaches Command with a DSO; VF Smith the Captain of AUBRETIA was also awarded the DSO and promoted to Commander RNR whilst still serving in the corvette, a very unusual rank for the post; Balme was awarded the DSC and became an acting Lieutenant-Commander in RENOWN eventually. The senior two officers could easily explain away their decorations, but what story did the Admiralty cook up for Balme to tell his mother?

3EG's haul so whetted the Admiralty's appetite for German coding and enciphering materials that deliberate operations were now planned against weather trawlers, which then netted other important keys and documents. As a result, in little over two years' time, the signal traffic of the German Navy was being read regularly and rapidly 'without significant interruption for the rest of the war'[5]

The resultant capacity for interpreting and forestalling enemy naval intentions became the great 'Ultra' secret, which had to be kept at all costs. The Battle still had to be won by the endurance of ships and by the perseverance of men, but some knowledge, of what dangers to avoid, saved both men and ships. Many were the ships and much was the individual expertise which would nurture Ultra, but it was 3EG and its first commander who provided its initial naval breakthrough.

NARCISSUS joins the great Atlantic game

The corvette's gestation had been a long one: ordered from Lewis's shipyard in August 1939, laid down in September 1940, she was only in the water and completed on 17th July 1941.[6] After commissioning she proceeded to Tobermory on the Isle of Mull off the west coast of Scotland to 'work up', as it was euphemistically described, under the eye of one of those make-believe martinets whom the sailors love to fear and whom the Navy produces with regularity. This was Commodore (really Vice-Admiral Rtd.) Sir Gilbert Stephenson, in command of the training base, HMS WESTERN ISLES. It has been my personal regret, only in long retrospect I hasten to add, to miss his ministrations:

joining a ship after it had undergone his scrutiny, as I did, I never experienced that delicious fear of wondering whether or not I had passed muster, nor the delirious joy of discovering that I had. Those who had have told me that Commodore Stephenson was a pussycat really, that there was always a twinkle behind the bark. Possibly; it is more likely that distance lends rosy memories. It was also a disappointment never now to be able to find any report on the work-up of NARCISSUS. It may be, as in the case of a mid-ocean inspection of NARCISSUS in 1944 when researched many years later, that all sea-commanders considered the trauma of operation exercises to be enough punishment in themselves; and that reports on their success or otherwise might have been damaging to morale and have had merely the dreary value of book-keeping. What has survived, however, is the outline of the 15-day programme devised by the 'Terror of Tobermory', as he came to be dubbed. This was to test each individual ship's efficiency in coping with the many challenges to come, from both the elements and the enemy.

Working Up Programmes, WESTERN ISLES

The programme for an escort ship arriving at Tobermory, in the evening prior to her fortnight's work-up, predicted an immediate interview for the commanding officer with the Commodore and his Chief of Staff. Next morning early, sundry staff officers would 'discuss' the ship's organization with the commanding officer, with the first lieutenant, gunnery, anti-submarine and depth-charge officers and with the cox'n and chief bosun's mate. That same morning the ship's armament would be inspected and other specialist staff officers would 'attend to effect repairs' – in all probability to ensure that thereafter no-one could blame the tools for poor work!

At 1130 there would be an instructional film for all ranks and ratings on 'Escort . . . Work'; by now Radar instruction would be under way. That first afternoon there was to be instruction on look-outs, on boatwork and seamanship, on gunnery and on submarine detection.

On the second day there were to be exercises and drills in communications, by wireless, by lamp and by flags. In the afternoon demonstrations and drills would take place on the guns, including rifles, on signalling, including with pyro-technics, and again with the anti-submarine equipment.

Day three saw the exercise of the two-pounder anti-aircraft 'pom-pom', this running concurrently with Radio/ Telephone exercises, and drills on the 'Hedgehog' (a forward-throwing mortar discharging multiple projectiles filled with the more powerful Torpex explosive – not fitted to NARCISSUS until 1942). The shift of the training staff's focus to accountancy and to the crew's teeth on the third day may by now have come as a blessed relief!

Day four saw these concerns repeated, with field training added for half the crew; and so on for fifteen days. This individual ship training ensured the professional upkeep of the instruments which would become available to an escort group's senior officer: when he ordered a particular manoeuvre, like boarding, towing, communicating etc., he would be able to depend upon a predictably proficient response from all his units. For teamwork in battle, on the other hand, he was going to have to rely upon the skills learned by his ships' captains at the Tactical Table Unit in Liverpool, famously directed by Captain Gilbert Roberts RN. Tobermory's value was evinced by the steadfastness and success of the ships which regularly graduated from its teachings throughout four years of the Battle: on 20th October 1944 Commodore Stephenson was able to report to Admiral Horton in Liverpool that the corvette CLOVER was the thousandth vessel to have been worked up at Tobermory.

NARCISSUS'S first attachment to the 4th Escort Group

The defeat of France and the enhanced ability of the German U-boat arm to penetrate deeply into the Atlantic caused problems for a British escort fleet constructed to operate over short distances. In 1942, in consequence, the system was for one set of escorts to start out with convoys from the Western Approaches of the UK; for another set to take them on from south of Iceland to Newfoundland and a further group to take them on to their western hemisphere destinations. Thus the first duty NARCISSUS found herself performing was that of delivering convoy ON9 to a Mid-Ocean Meeting Point (MOMP) and then returning to the UK, having met convoy HX145 at 55°46' North, 25°02' West. This rather unsatisfactory reciprocating relay race across the Atlantic, with a convoy of freighters as the baton being passed from one escort group to another, was to last for another seven months; more economical use of escorts' sea-time would be achieved when the endurance of corvettes was improved and when the new frigates came down the slipways.

So NARCISSUS was at first integrated into 4EG, one of the two groups which constituted the Clyde Escort Force on 21st August 1941. There she joined BOADICEA (Commander HP Henderson RN) and the other old destroyers BEAGLE, SALISBURY and WINCHELSEA. Her first sister corvette was HEATHER, which was rather remarkably under the command of a Lt. Commander RN. Convoy ON9 comprised 51 merchant ships and included three aircraft-catapulting freighters; this 'flock' was under the leadership of Commodore Errol Manners RNR in SICILIAN PRINCESS; three naval trawlers assisted the 'shepherds'.

So, on 25th August two of the destroyers and two of the corvettes left the westbound ON9 and took over the east-bound HX145, which comprised 83 ships including four catapulting (CAM) ships and the rescue ship ZAAFAREN. All were led by Admiral (Rtd.) BS Thesiger in SS HEKTORIA (which ship he would subsequently declare to be '. . . not suitable for a Commodore.'). ZAAFAREN, fitted with the direction-finding (HF/DF) equipment which served her secondary task of detecting enemy radio transmissions, heard a nearby U-boat; within ten minutes SS SAUGOR had been torpedoed. The trawler SEAGULL searched for survivors, but unsuccessfully, and the destroyer SALISBURY lost a man overboard. After these mishaps, the ships of HX145 sailed on to their several destinations.

When 4EG had been approaching this convoy in mid-ocean in daylight on the 25th, BEAGLE considered that she could see smoke from its funnels from 35 miles away. She reported this in writing for the serious problem that it was: obviously other forms of evasive action would be rendered pointless, if U-boats merely had to sit on the surface in clear weather and make towards any nearby smoke. This was a problem which was to plague convoys for a long time to come.

Convoys ON14 and SC42: September 1941

BOADICEA was again in charge of 4EG when the next 'halfway' convoy, 47 ships at 6.4 knots under Rear Admiral AC Candy in KING STEPHEN, set out on 7th September. This time the Commodore was pleased with his ship and subsequently asked that the ship's master be commended to his owners. Two Free French corvettes, FFS LOBELIA and FFS RENONCULE, now joined NARCISSUS for the first time. The merchantmen were intact when 4EG left them at 56°25' N 24° 50' W on 14th September, but then dispersed on the 15th and lost two of their number.

The return convoy, SC42, had had an even worse time before it came under the protection of its Western Approaches escort group: 67 ships with an average speed of 6½ knots under Commodore WB Mackenzie in EVERLEIGH, had set out from Nova Scotia at the end of August, had endured five days of northerly gales and then had lost 17 ships torpedoed between the 6th and 11th September, mostly at night. The Canadian escorts noticed the great daring of the U-boats, sometimes surfacing in daylight and emerging in the middle of the convoy. The Commodore's patience was severely taxed by ships which were allegedly abandoned when still salvageable, in one case leaving the confidential books on board. The careless showing of lights also became a problem in this convoy: one ship only put out her light after one of her neighbours in the next column aimed five rounds of rifle-fire at her; this became the threatened punishment for the offence. The Commodore became so incensed at the excessive smoke made that he proposed to the C-in-C, Western Approaches, that ships which made too much smoke should 'be detached' by the Commodore. Since expulsion from the convoy would frequently turn out to be a death sentence for the ship concerned, the C-in-C swiftly vetoed the suggestion.

In compensation, two Canadian corvettes sank U-501 and rescued 26 German survivors. Only one more ship was lost after SALISBURY and NARCISSUS joined the escort on 16th September.

ONS19 and HX151: September/October 1941

The next slow, outward convoy comprised 45 ships, including two CAM ships. The escorts from Greenock were now led by BEAGLE, whose captain was the very experienced and successful Commander RT White, RN, DSO and Bar. When in command of HMS ANTELOPE in 1940 his ship had sunk U-41 in February and U-31 in November; this doughty warrior was to survive until 1995. The slow convoy lost one tanker and suffered an autumnal gale, but this time did not disperse until it had reached 54°W, i.e. well within the shelter of air cover; 4EG of course had turned it over at 22°20' W.

From the MOMP 4EG brought back without loss HX151,

a rather faster convoy of 47 laden ships including four CAM ships at 9.25 knots, clearly with the wind behind them.

ONS26 and SC49: October 1941

Before overtaking the fairly fast (7.72 knots) outward-bound ONS26 (37 ships, including the rescue ship ZAMALEK and two CAM ships, Commodore G. Mackworth, CMG, DSO, in MANCHESTER MERCHANT), NARCISSUS and LOBELIA carried out firing and anti-submarine exercises off Ireland, probably with the Admiralty yacht MAGOG and a tame submarine. The subsequent convoy suffered no loss and seems to have been well and variously covered from the air: by a Hudson on the 15th October, a Sunderland and a Whitney on the 17th, a Whitney on the 18th, a Wellington on the 19th and by three Catalinas and a Hudson on the 20th. If only all convoys had been this fortunate; the recognition skills of the ships' lookouts must have been well tested on this occasion. Escorting was turned over at the MOMP to an American group of 6 destroyers led by USS MAYO.

SC49 was duly met for the return journey by 4EG at 1000hrs on 23rd May in 20°W. Apart from some grumbling in the reports about indiscipline among wireless operators and casual station-keeping by officers-of-the-watch in the merchant ships, there were few problems with this convoy. It is little wonder that the ships showed a '... general tendency to hang back, especially at night ...' in view of what had happened to convoy SC42 only the previous month, when several of the leading ships of columns had been among the many casualties.

All convoys were, of course, valuable and SC49 was even more so: its 31 ships included five tankers and seven 'specials' which, in the event, all arrived safely.

ONS33 and HX158: November 1941

Commodore EO Cochrane in FRAMLINGHAM COURT led out 60 ships at what was to prove an average speed of 5.7 knots and on 4th November 4EG commenced escort duty from the UK to Iceland. Once again, but after the takeover by the mid-ocean escorts, the Commodore was to have problems with a ship showing navigation lights at night and this was only resolved by a corvette opening machine-gun fire against the offender.

The Commodore also recommended to the Admiralty that the streaming of anti-aircraft balloons by ships be discontinued, because all theirs were '. . . blown away or exploded . . .' Unlike the draconian proposal by the Commodore of SC42, this suggestion must have found favour, for the first balloons I ever saw streamed by ships were when crossing the Channel for D-Day 2½ years later. These early reports also occasionally mention 'kites'; although ingenious, they must have given much trouble for limited protection.

The Canadian group which took over from 4EG at the MOMP on 11th November included the ill-fated British corvette POLYANTHUS, of whom more later; the group had already had a rough time of it in a gale south of Iceland, HMCS ST. LAURENT getting her topmast carried away and her motorboat holed.

The homeward-bound HX158 was even more valuable than SC49 had been: 7 'specials' and 24 tankers among the 40 ships, which also included a CAM ship and the rescue ship PERTH. Prior to the takeover from its US escorts at the MOMP, 4EG's corvettes swept a path ahead of the convoy. Thereafter the precious cargoes were delivered safely to the UK.

ON40 and SC56: November/December 1941

When 4EG was taking ON40 westwards, one of the regular trawlers, HMT LADY MADELEINE, reported by Radio/Telephone on 28th November in 59°N, 15°'W that she had sighted a conning-tower, had fired two rounds from her 4" gun, had attempted to ram and had dropped two successive patterns of five depth-charges each, the latter five set to go off at a depth of only 50 feet; unhappily the latter only succeeded in putting her own electronics and Asdic out of action. Despite BEAGLE, HEATHER and COMMANDANT DETROYAT (a Free French substitute for the usual two on this occasion) coming to her support, the full gale which had blown since the 26th prevented the little ship from reaping the harvest she so richly deserved.

The detailed account of the R/T exchanges during this incident gives some insight into both the scepticism of the Senior Officer in BEAGLE and the simple code-names used in what had to be plain-language, tactical communications between ships. When addressing the trawler captain over the R/T, the S.O. found it prudent and quicker to say: ' "Mad", this is "Hound" '. The first thing he wanted to know was if the trawler were sure that the sighting was not of a whale. LADY MADELEINE hotly denied this, having seen the actual periscope. When later addressing NARCISSUS over the R/T with more erudition than brevity, the S.O. called her 'Reflection': only an eavesdropping U-boat totally ignorant of Greek mythology would have been deceived by that one.

NARCISSUS too was suspected of seeing things: a Radar contact was rejected, even by Captain (D)'s unconsciously erudite report from his Greenock headquarters, as: '. . . probably a reflection from the funnel.'

The Canadian escort group which arrived to take over ON40 at the MOMP included the Free French corvettes ACONIT and MIMOSA. The former was destined to become a distinguished member of B3 Escort Group; the latter was now instructed to carry the head of the

Free French Navy, Admiral Muselier, from Iceland to Newfoundland. Clearly the United States were not monitoring their Ally's wireless transmissions, otherwise this signal might have alerted them to the fact that the North American islands of St Pierre and Miquelon were about to be rallied to De Gaulle, strictly against American wishes.

On 4th December 4EG left Iceland to perform the return leg of its duty; it took more than a day for the Group to reach SC56. This slow eastward convoy of 45 ships, Commodore GN Jones in RARANGA, had been hove to twice in continuously bad weather and could only achieve an onward progressive of 6.4 knots. When the escorts joined, in 19°W, they were immediately set the task of rounding up stragglers; 15 ships did not rejoin and one, SCOTTISH TRADER, was never seen again.

In antithesis to the crustiness often displayed by Commodores, this one was fulsome in his praise of the master of RARANGA, Captain WBS Starr, who had been a prisoner in the GRAF SPEE and in the ALTMARK, as had his Chief Officer. It was a measure of the gritty resilience of such members of the merchant service that they continued to face the dangers of the sea, when many might have thought them to have faced enough already.

ONS47 and HX165: December/January 1941/42

BEAGLE had now left the Group and BOADICEA was unable to conduct the next convoy westwards, because of damage incurred after grounding in Loch Ewe. Temporary leadership therefore devolved upon a frequent partner, ROXBOROUGH; but this was to be her last Western Approaches duty. After ONS47 she went on to join the local escort force in Newfoundland; in little over a year's time, however, the fragility of her class would be exposed by the North Atlantic. So the four corvettes, HEATHER, NARCISSUS, LOBELIA, COMMANDANT DETROYAT and the rescue ship COPELAND went directly from ONS47 to the eastbound HX165. BOADICEA never did find ONS47, but caught up on Christmas Eve and took over the leadership of the escorts. HX165 turned out to be satisfactory neither for inter-allied co-operation nor for NARCISSUS: in the first incident, at the MOMP, American destroyers fired at a British plane which was trying to establish contact. The plane dropped recognition flares but the US gunnery controller, nervous because he felt the plane was too close, thought the flares were machine-gun fire. Fortunately his responding 'friendly fire' missed.

There were also worries expressed about finding the meeting point. In theory, the advantages of having two sets of escorts in the vicinity, at the most dangerous part of the ocean, may have seemed attractive. In practice, the difficulties and dangers inherent in the possibilities of missing the MOMP, either through bad weather or by navigational error, outweighed the potential benefits and were probably factors in the imminent abandonment of a mid-ocean handover.

The second incident, which led to embarrassment for NARCISSUS, all started with a visual signal from the Commodore, Vice-Admiral (Rtd.) DF Moir in PACIFIC EXPLORER. The rear ship of the fifth column, SS SHANTUNG, had dropped behind in the early hours of Christmas Day, had been on fire and the crew had abandoned ship. NARCISSUS was then detailed to stand by the stricken vessel. Half a gale was blowing and, despite zigzagging astern for two days, no sign was found of her. However, a Swedish ship, met 20 miles north of the line of the convoy's track, signalled that she had survivors aboard from SHANTUNG. At about that time, the tug TENACITY arrived to tow SHANTUNG and the two British ships searched back along the course given by the Swede for five hours at twelve knots without success. Aircraft of Coastal Command finally found SHANTUNG on 2nd January 1942 and sank her, since she had become a hazard to shipping. Captain (D) back in Greenock would put an ominous gloss on the subsequent report: 'The SHANTUNG affair appears to have been a most regrettable one.' The remaining 47 ships sailed on and were delivered safely.

ON54: January 1942

The same five team-mates met the outward-bound ON54 off Barra Head on 7th January. Adverse winds delayed the convoy's arrival at the MOMP, but BOADICEA had to leave early in order to refuel in Iceland and NARCISSUS was ordered to accompany the rescue ship DEWSBURY there as she had run out of coal! BOADICEA had a turbulent time at this point, broaching to and losing a man overboard whilst avoiding a collision with a group of American destroyers; then she was blinded by coastal searchlights and fired on by coastal batteries in Iceland.

The Canadian group which took over the escort of ON54 included the British Flower-class corvette DIANTHUS; the two British corvettes, DIANTHUS and POLYANTHUS had supplied a cheerful presence to the Newfoundland Escort Force and were known as the 'Anthus' sisters: 'Di' and 'Polly'. Sadly, NARCISSUS would see the heart knocked out of the relationship eighteen months later, when DIANTHUS's former Captain, Commander Bridgeman RNR, disappeared with his new command, the frigate ITCHEN, and POLYANTHUS would be sunk with scarcely a trace.

After delivering the westbound ON54, 4EG returned to the Clyde independently, because the Admiralty had ordered the dispersal of the incoming SC63 on 13th January before it could reach the MOMP. Severe gales had compelled it to heave on to 9th January; it had been battered again on 11th and was finally dispersed in winds of 117 knots, a hurricane wind-force which went right off the Beaufort scale. One ship to have had a bad time in this convoy was the Yugoslav NIKOLINA MATROVIC, the effects of which would probably drive one of her engineers over the brink of mental breakdown during the subsequent convoy, as we shall see.

ONS60 and SC66: January/February 1942

The next convoy 4EG took westwards was also scattered by a gale from January 27th until February 1st; the bright side was that this probably inhibited enemy attacks until after ON60 had been turned over to a Canadian group on 2nd February. Forming part of this group was the Free French corvette ALYSSE and she was torpedoed in position 45°50'N, 44°48'W on February 8th. Her whole bow section up to the bridge and mast was demolished, but two of her Canadian consorts managed to take off 34 survivors. Two days after the turnover of ONS60 4EG, together with the rescue ship RATHLIN, met the eastbound SC66, comprising only 29 ships, 78 miles further south. The handover was again from a Canadian group, which had experienced fog on their section of the transatlantic journey. In that fog two Greek freighters, 4th ships in each of the 2nd and 3rd columns, had collided and the crew of the AEGEUS, a grain carrier, had abandoned ship. The Senior Officer of the Canadians, in HMCS BURNHAM, considered the AEGEUS to be seaworthy, found the rescued crew in SS CRAGPOOL, sent an armed party aboard the latter and 'persuaded' the crew to return to AEGEUS. Commodore HC Birnie in BALTROVER commended BURNHAM for saving the grain carrier for the war effort. At 08°00'W the convoy split and NARCISSUS and COMMANDANT DETROYAT let away the Loch Ewe Section.

SC68 and ON70: February/March 1942

The rhythm of escorting, or 'cycles' as it is called elsewhere (i.e., for 4EG, taking roughly every seventh ON or ONS convoy westwards to the MOMP and then meeting every seventh HX or SC in mid-Atlantic and bringing it home) was modified in February 1942.

After bringing in SC66, 4EG rushed out again to bring in the next but one of the Sydney, Cape Breton departures, SC68, meeting it on 16th February. Difficulties of turnover and the occasional need to disperse convoys had to be contained. The epic events of 1941, with the United States and Russia being forced into the War, created new opportunities for the British in the Atlantic, principal among which was the availability of the newly-established American naval base at Argentia in Newfoundland. It was therefore probably to the relief of all concerned that SC68 was the last half-way duty that NARCISSUS was to carry out; it was also the last convoy for her under the aegis of the old 'B' class destroyers of 4EG, which were now destined for the Arctic and Murmansk.

Henceforth the convoys were to be escorted all the way to the Western Ocean Meeting Point (WESTOMP) by the same escort group. The return convoy would also, therefore, be escorted continuously without the interruption of a mid-ocean exchange. ON70 was thus escorted by the new British 3rd Escort Group (B3), led for the time being by the Polish destroyer ORP PIORUN, but with Commander HP Henderson RN, transferred from his previous command BOADICEA, as Senior Officer. LOBELIA, HEATHER and NARCISSUS remained as the nucleus of the Clyde Escort Force and were supported, for the outward journey only, by two Canadian corvettes. Gales continued to hamper the passage but, between 26th February and 10th March the same escorts stayed to shepherd and to cajole the inevitable stragglers all the way to 45°42'N, 45°42'W. HEATHER then headed for the American base at Argentia, in Placentia Bay on the southern Avalon peninsula and the rest of the Group went to savour the hospitality of St John's, capital of New-foundland.

SC75: March 1942

On 21st B3 Group joined 28 ships in 46°26'N, 52°09'W under Commodore Sir Raymond Fitzmaurice in DORELIAN. The Polish escort leader now had the temporary support of an American destroyer, USS WOOLSEY, in place of the two Canadians. Also providing HF/DF services and rescue facilities at the back of the convoy was an old friend, RATHLIN.

The fact that the formal enemy failed to put in an appearance did not diminish the other risks to be faced. Convoy SC75 still had to negotiate two such hazards. On March 26th the first concerned an Irish independent streamer bound for St John's. Even though she was found to be genuine when challenged, the convoy altered 40° to port as soon as the Irish ship was over the horizon, as a precaution against her reporting the convoy's position; and then made a correction to the course later. The second hazard was posed by that 'auld enemy' the sea: two cases of 'violent insanity' had to be taken by escorts from ships in the convoy, one from INGMAN and another from NIKOLINA MATROVIC. Both the violently disturbed men were engineers; which is not to be wondered at, considering the chances of survival of men stationed deep in the engine- or boiler-rooms of a freighter, if torpedoed. One of the two ships was that Yugoslav reported as suffering from the hurricane which struck SC63 during the previous January.

In his report, Sir Raymond was another who belied that famous irritability of Commodores by praising and commending both the escort commander and the captain and crew of his 'flagship' DORELIAN. On 1st April the convoy split at 09°W and NARCISSUS carried off the Loch Ewe portion.

ONS84: April 1942

The second full-length outward-bound convoy was small and slow: the 23 ships were intended to advance at a speed of 7½ knots, but could only manage an average of 6.53 knots. The longer time through the critical zone in mid-Atlantic did not, however, result in casualties, as might have been feared, for this convoy reached the other side without loss. B3 had secured the services, for the passage of ONS84 only, of the slightly newer destroyer FIREDRAKE. For the next ten months the Group would be led by one of the modern 'H' class, a repaired veteran of Dunkirk. This convoy also saw the return, now on a more permanent basis, of B3's second Free French corvette, RENONCULE. On arrival at WESTOMP on the 23rd, NARCISSUS left to make her first visit to the American base at Argentia.

HX188: May 1942

Not only did HMS HARVESTER take over leadership of the Group for the first time on 5th May 1942, but the Polish destroyer ORP GARLAND also now made her first appearance in the 4EG/B3 record. They, NARCISSUS, the two French corvettes and MIGNONETTE all joined HX188 in the square 47°N, 50°W (there was some divergence between the reports by the Commodore and the Senior Officer as to the exact position!) at 1400 hours on 6th May. The 28 ships under Commodore WEB Magee, DSO, in TILAPA would achieve an overall speed of 8.79 knots.

Air cover for the convoy, between 3rd and 7th May and between 11th and 14th May, left the vulnerable gap of four days, which the enemy could normally be counted upon to exploit. The new Senior Officer, Commander AA Tait RN now laid the foundation for his subsequent reputation as a 'smeller-out' of U-boats, much as primitive doctors are reputed to locate witches (and with not dissimilar methods, both he and they relying upon secret information, not available to their admiring audience). On the 11th Tait 're-commended' to the Commodore a drastic night alteration of compass course, in view of signals received from the Admiralty and of HF/DF bearings obtained of the enemy's transmissions. This manoeuvre, combined with a sweep astern by a selection of escorts after dark, managed to give the U-boats the slip and HX188 sailed on unscathed.

On reaching 08°W in British waters on 14th May, NARCISSUS became due for her first refit, when new technology would be installed and the ship would be made more suited to the long transatlantic passages, for which she had not at first been designed. When she came out of Govan dockyard, she would find herself to be a member of a more settled team.

References

[1] For this account of Lemp's fate, see J. Costello and T. Hughes, 1980, *The Battle of the Atlantic*, Fontana, pp. 148–9; unfortunately, they offer no precise reference. Alternatively refer to Ronald Lewin, 1978, *Ultra goes to War*, Hutchinson, p. 205. Otherwise see David Kahn, 1991, *Seizing the Enigma*, Souvenir Press, pp. 14, 166–168. Also ADM 1/11133: the fact that this success is designated in the public record as 'Operation Primrose' causes me to suspect that the capture of the Enigma machine from U-110 was not entirely fortuitous.

[2] ADM 199/2058.

[3] Correlli Barnett, 1991, *Engage the Enemy More Closely*, Hodder & Staughton, p. 267.

[4] ADM 199/1985; also ADM 199/2099.

[5] Kahn, *op. cit.*, p. 242.

[6] R. A. Ruegg, 1991, unpublished outline 'HMS NARCISSUS (K74)'.

Apart from the references above, unpublished information for this chapter has been drawn from the following files in the Public Recored Office at Kew, London: classification ADM 199/55, 56, 582, 684, 713, 716, 718, 729, 1145, 1147, 1729, 2058, 2099; and from ADM 237/586, 591, 597, 603 and 617.

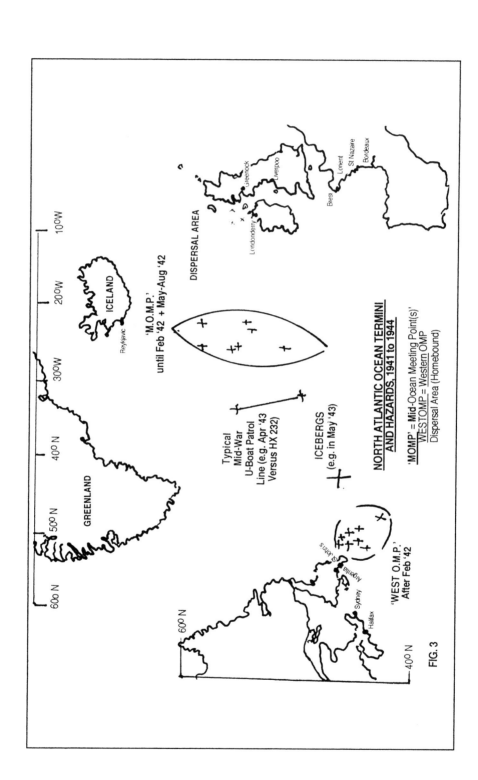

FIG. 3

CHAPTER 4

The Summer Respite of 1942: an opportunity for learning

Whilst NARCISSUS languished in drylock in Govan, B3 Group, comprising HARVESTER, PIORUN, ORCHIS and RENONCULE with PRIMROSE as a one-way consort, had gone out to meet 31 ships (Convoy ONS98, Commodore Goldsmith in INGLETON) at 55°N, 22°W, i.e. well out into the Atlantic. The Senior Officer, Commander A. A. Tait, RN, DSO, took passage in ORCHIS, presumably for experience of life at sea in a corvette.

After the Iceland escort had left, they all settled down to an uneventful voyage, enlivened only by the sudden appearance of an independent ship, who was taken for a commerce raider. She turned out to be Swedish, however, and was allowed to proceed, the Group breaking away for Argentia on 7 June.

HX194

Sailing from Argentia on 16 June, less PRIMROSE but with former colleague LOBELIA restored, B3 Group took over 31 ships (Commodore Denis in SS CORNERBROOK) from an ex-AMERICAN 'four-stacker', HMS ROXBOROUGH, who was so soon to suffer the savagery of the sea. She now belonged to the local Newfoundland Escort Force, whose task was probably regarded by the newly re-organized ocean escorts as a sinecure, since local escorts operated under the protection of land-based air-cover between St John's and New York. If so, that opinion would have been unjust, because the first few months of 1942 had provided the U-boat crews with their second 'happy time'; this was the name the Germans gave to the opportunity to sink unescorted ships off the southeastern United States' coast almost at will, air-cover or no.

It was also, of course, that German concentration of effort upon the sea-trade of the newly combatant Americans which gave our own shipping and convoys something of a reprieve. In all probability, for example, my own un-trammelled arrival from Brazil, by independently-routed passenger liner via Freetown in February, had owed a great deal to the shift of German attention to American inshore traffic by then.

Even by June 1942, B3 Group's return journey with HX194 to the UK from Newfoundland was again virtually without incident. The only encounter was with convoy NA11, trans-porting troops. HMS BITER was in company and flying off covering aircraft; she was one of the new escort carriers intended to close the mid-Atlantic gap for us but, for now and rightly, the protection of bodies took precedence over the protection of freight. Until after the North African land-ings had been completed, North Atlantic traffic would have to make do with air-cover provided first by those few merchant ships fitted with one-time Hurricane fighters cata-pulted off the forecastle (CAM ships); and subsequently by merchant aircraft carriers, with their four Swordfish parked on an open deck (MAC ships).

Only when HX194 reached the south side of Rockall was it deemed safe for the freighters to continue without their ocean escorts and B3 then left for the Tyne.

Norwegian survivors on board Narcissus

HMS Trawler Northern Sky*:*
Note Convoy on horizon

*CAM Ship, Hurricane fighter
poised to launch*

Convoys OS35, ON121, HX202: the relearning of convoy discipline

Coming out of refit, NARCISSUS did not immediately return to her Group but was temporarily attached to the 43rd Escort Group, which was heading southward with OS35. The corvette was soon in danger of running out of fuel and returned to base. After some waiting around, much to the frustration of the inexperienced and naive among us (I was soon told by the more war-weary members of the wardroom not to fidget, we would get to sea quite soon enough), we started off northwards. B3 Group now comprised HARVESTER, PIORUN, NARCISSUS, ORCHIS and RENONCULE; this time the guest corvette making up our numbers was HEATHER. We met ON121 (Commodore, Vice Admiral ML Goldsmith in SS WATERLAND) well into the Atlantic again, at Longitude 25°36'West. It comprised 34 ships, including 8 tankers, and achieved a respectable average speed of 8.16 knots. Since the U-boats still seemed to be recuperating from the hangover induced by the many 'happy hours' they had recently enjoyed off the eastern seaboard of America, our trade-route appeared to be inviolate.

It did seem, at this time, that the lull encouraged the more fire-eating Commodores to ginger up their patient merchantmen. The current one was no exception; he probably had been advised that the lull would not last. He wrote the sort of letter that, in happier times, might have appeared in the correspondence columns of a national broadsheet and might have been signed by 'Disgusted of Tunbridge Wells'. With scant diplomacy the Commodore reported the '. . . disgraceful example which the Master of this ship showed to a collection of ships of seven nationalities. I have never experienced such insubordination in all my time as Commodore . . . etc. etc.'

This reprimand was in respect of a tanker which, 25 miles before reaching the western dispersal point, had broken away from the convoy and had proceeded alone. Signals from the Commodore and a personal request from alongside by the local escort (HMS WITCH) failed to deter this classic display of independence. It could not have assuaged the Commodore's apoplexy that the tanker's original convoy position was that of fourth ship in the Commodore's own column, so she must have steamed boldly past him at the start of her 'romp' towards their mutual destination. Admiral Goldsmith addressed his adverse report, in the first instance, to the tanker's owners, for which he received a polite 'bottle' from the relevant government department ashore for not going through the proper administrative channels. The tanker captain eventually explained that the convoy speed was so slow that his ship had started shaking enough to make bits fall off the bridge. He suavely added, Nelson-fashion, that he had seen no signals and that the escort ship had merely told him that his ship would, presumably in consequence of his naughtiness, be the last to pass through the entry channel to his destination. It had often seemed to the escort ships that the merchantmen were mute sheep to be defended from the wolf-packs and bullied into line. Clearly they were not; their coming together evidently created a cauldron of emotions.

The return convoy, HX202, was even speedier with a prevailing wind behind it, achieving an average overall of 9.31 knots. Discipline for the 41 ships was not eased up merely because the enemy was showing no interest: the Commodore (Rear Admiral Errol Manners RN [Rtd.] in CAVINA) reported SS BRANT COUNTY for 'roaming'. Poor BRANT COUNTY: seven months later we saw her cargo of ammunition explode into the shape of a peacock's tail a thousand feet high.

ONS126 and HX207

The same faithful six shepherded a small convoy of 22 ships safely into the teeth of a gale on 1 September 1942 and then through a concentration of U-boats on the 6th without being spotted. Half the ships were European (1 Greek, 2 Dutch, 5 Norwegian, 2 Swedish, 1 Belgian) and, naturally enough on this westward journey, most were in ballast. The heavy weather made it difficult for some to keep up, so that this already slow convoy barely made an average rate of advance of 6 knots. The frustrated Commodore (F. H. Taylor in the Norwegian RENA) was finally able to turn his ire, not this time upon an erring ship's captain but, on to shipping controllers ashore. Ten miles outside New York ON126 had to perform an emergency 45° turn to port to avoid another convoy: 'Had the weather been thick,' reported the Commodore, 'the two convoys would have collided . . . gross negligence on someone's part.' All the Commodore got for his pains was a bland response from the US authorities, relayed via the British Admiralty Delegation in Washington, to the effect that the obstruction had been '. . . an escorted group of ships out of their plotted position.'

The two destroyers and the four corvettes left Argentia on 15 September, joining HX207 the next afternoon. The inaction of that autumn now also seemed to affect our Senior Officer, the normally equable 'Harry' Tait: three Canadian corvettes came and went over several days, generating too much radio/telephone and wireless/telegraphy traffic for his liking in an area apparently full of U-boats; his report reflected the strain upon him. Commodores as well as senior officers in those relatively tranquil months seemed like those 'ladies' in the familiar couplet: '. . . in our hours of ease, uncertain, coy and hard to please.'

The 38 merchantmen of HX207 bounded along at an average of 9.38 knots, a speed that seems to have so bemused the leader of the Belfast section that he incurred the following official reprimand from his Commodore, Vice Admiral Austin, RN [Rtd.]: 'The Rear Commodore, Belfast section, . . . Captain [. . .] is not recommended as Rear or Vice Commodore. When detached – early to save daylight – having suggested that he increase speed – he did not do so – and led his portion across my bows so that the rear of his columns became entangled with the two Mersey columns and, had it been dark, a very dangerous situation would have arisen. As it was I had to signal rear ships of his column in very strong language to disentangle them and send them on at full speed. I do not think the Belfast Commodore can ever have glanced astern to see what was happening or how his ships were struggling . . .' Apart from being a minor example of the irascibility of Commodores, this incident is curious in that convoys were normally pre-disposed in such a way as to enable whole sections to peel off in the appropriate direction at the dispersal point, normally without incommoding the rest of the convoy. Inward, eastbound convoys would have all ships dispersing to, say, Loch Ewe and northabout the British Isles for the east coast of Britain, in the port columns; ships for Ireland and Belfast in the starboard columns; ships for the Clyde left of centre, and so on. This sensible arrangement was precisely intended to avoid that daring manoeuvring which so unnerved Admiral Austin.

ON136 and SC106

Convoy ON136 was so featureless that it seems to have left no trace at all of its passage; had we but known it, this convoy marked the end of the lull for us. Henceforth either the sea or the enemy would make life very unpleasant for the next twelve months.

SC106 (Commodore, Rear Admiral DM Bedford in WEARWOOD) was not meant to be a slow convoy ('SC' stood for its port of origin, Sydney, Cape Breton in Canada) but its rate of advance was well below 7 knots. Its 22 ships had difficulty coping with a westerly gale which developed into a hurricane; by 26 October some ships were heaving to, as a preferable alternative to broaching to, in the violent stern sea; but this obviously cut down the rate of advance eastwards.

B3 Group took over from three Canadian corvettes of the

local escort group outside St John's on 23 February and already some of the merchantmen were straggling and had to be chivvied back into line. One of these stragglers was the Panamanian HH ROGERS. This time the weather protected her from the enemy; four months later, again in our charge, similarly foul weather would not protect her from being torpedoed.

ORP GARLAND had now taken over the Polish spot in the ongoing danse macabre around the convoys; and HEATHER had taken her luck elsewhere, now that our regular Free Frenchmen, ACONIT and LOBELIA were back. On 2 December the Senior Officer of B3 advised the Commodore to alter course 28° to starboard to avoid a perceived U-boat threat; having done so successfully and having reached air-cover at 56°26'N, 08°32'W, the ocean escort left for the Clyde.

A tyro's time for learning

If the summer and autumn of 1942 had enabled the larger lessons of convoy discipline to be re-learned, it also gave one nineteen-year-old time to learn some social lessons about life in a corvette. The first lesson was that, if you are the junior member and/or the most recently arrived of any human work group, you are likely to take up the role and the tasks of the 'dogsbody'; i.e. you will quickly be allocated all the routine tasks no-one else wants. On arrival in NARCISSUS in June 1942, therefore, I was appointed Captain's secretary. Ostensibly this did not turn out to be too arduous, since the Captain seemed to write as few official reports as possible; and the only organization that seemed to write to him, as opposed to sending him signals, was the suburb of Manchester, Denton, which had 'adopted' the ship in order to send the crew 'comforts'.

Learning the facts of life

What did turn out to be an insufferable chore was the duty of ship's censor: all the ratings sending their mail home through the ship's postman had to have it censored. The purpose seemed to be to prevent mention of ships' names, ports of call, losses, technical details, etc. Since most of the sailors merely wished to communicate either shy endearments or anticipations to their wives and sweethearts, censorship seemed a monumental waste of time, to say nothing of an obscene intrusion into personal privacy.

I was certainly not the right person either by virtue of age or preparation to be made privy to their private thoughts and relationships. Not that I would have dreamed of discussing what I was compelled to read: I was too horrified, in my puritanism, to repeat what appeared to be going on in the minds of all who surrounded me. As for security, I would have been incapable of detecting any simple code for passing information which the resourceful sailory may have devised. I now discover, from a current publication, that this is precisely what they did. Posting a letter on shore was not an option for the men; as can be seen from a slightly bloodcurdling notice in red which greeted each ship as she arrived for the working-up period in Tobermory. Any letter posted ashore would merely be returned to the ship by the civilian censors, for disciplinary action. The zeal of these latter was never in doubt: they did not merely blacken out the offending words, they cut them out with scissors. My own letter to my parents in Rio de Janeiro arrived looking like lace-paper.

I began to see the censorship task as a sadistic conspiracy to fill in my time both at sea and in harbour in order to keep me 'out of mischief'. The most attractive memories which have remained from all that time were the acronyms appended to many of the letters: S.W.A.L.K. was an affecting one, 'Sealed With A Loving Kiss'. A bolder one, 'H.O.L.L.A.N.D.' meant, I was reliably informed, 'Have On Less Lace And No Drawers'. My informant in most matters of the heart was Leading Ordnance Artificer Greene, a 'dayman' who maintained the guns. During the afternoon watches at sea (I kept a standing watch, noon to 4 p.m. daily; and then midnight to 4 a.m., known as the 'graveyard watch' – another sadistic conspiracy!), on the pretext of servicing the Oerlikon quickfirers on the bridge, Greene would contrive to keep me abreast of episodes in his life-history. No amount of discouragement would prevent him from dispensing nuggets from his trove of anecdotes, which stretched from his childhood as a Dr Barnardo's boy to his current amorous adventures ashore.

Had this secular confessional interfered with watch-keeping (there were other lookouts on the bridge and he was adept at picking the quiet moments), or had the recounting of an often arduous youth been tinged with complaint, I am sure that I would have found the courage to stem the flow. But the unfailing good humour and an evident urge for self-revelation kept me buttonholed by this latterday Ancient Mariner; although, in fact, he could only have had a few years advantage over me.

Leading Artificer Greene's interior life was probably no different from that of most of the crew; it was just that from him I was privileged to get a more complete picture, whereas from the others I got, at the most, snapshots. In a nautical sub-culture I was probably placed in that limbo reserved for a midshipman (which is what I really should have been): the sort of limbo whose occupants are too remote to take liberties with but too young to have to take seriously.

Instinctual behaviour re-asserts itself in mid-Atlantic

One flash of insight vouchsafed to me in those early days involved one of the strong men of the lower deck. This was the Chief Bos'n's Mate, a large red-haired freckle-faced man who drove the daily work of the upper deck, partly by example and partly by physical presence. One relatively calm forenoon in mid-Atlantic I had to pass by the Petty Officers' Mess, something watchkeeping officers rarely did, unlike the daily inspection of the forward mess decks of junior ratings. Petty Officers jealously guarded their separately favoured position as the backbone of naval discipline. I had been deputed by the First Lieutenant to invigilate the daily issue of rum (a cheerful moment in the daily routine, now sadly abolished); I was accompanying the Cox'n, who occupied the enviable position of senior Chief Petty Officer aboard, as well as being director of the rum ration. The Petty Officers' mess was right aft, as was the victualling room where the rum was kept.

Looking into the Mess as I passed, I was astonished to see the Chief Bos'n's Mate in his bunk at this time of day, stirring slightly and groaning. The sight of this huge man behaving in so uncharacteristic a fashion must have unnerved me, for I forgot all discretion; he could not be sea-sick, he must be ill.

'What's the matter with him!' I blurted out to a sardonic Cox'n. 'His wife is having a baby, back in England,' he replied with only the glimmer of a smile.

I was disinclined to believe him until, twenty years later, I learned of the *couvade,* a ritual mimicry of a wife's birth-pangs carried out by her husband in certain societies; in their case the male is presumed only to be pretending to be in pain. His motive is said to be the establishment of his paternal rights. But here in mid-Atlantic was a male who needed no such motive, who probably had everything to lose from a display of frailty, yet whose marital instincts were so impressive over all that distance. His secret was safe with me – until now, when all it can do him is honour.

Romance among the depth-charges

Another insight into the problems posed by the separation of the sexes in this all-male sub-society was offered to me, on another occasion when I was away from the formality of the ship's bridge. Passing along the port waist on the upper deck, I rounded the first of the two depth-charge throwers just in time to see, at a range of about 4 feet, one of the long-service Able Seamen (i.e. one who had already served 13 years in the Navy) kiss the ear of one of the prettier Ordinary Seamen on board. The only person not to be disconcerted was the Able Seaman, who stared blandly back at me. The Ordinary Seaman, no older than I, had been standing rigidly to attention with his cap on through this momentary experience; and the look of bafflement on his face matched my own. No word passed between the three of us and I passed on my way.

I had been aware, of course, that boys at school were liable to direct their burgeoning sexuality at one another in the absence of girls. A 'scandal' had been alleged in the 1920s at my school, which I could not fail to know about because it was liberally publicized by Alex Waugh in his *magnum opus* 'The Loom of Youth'. In consequence the school's authorities came down very heavily upon anything remotely sexual that might have given rise to further concern. One sporting hero at the school during my time there, for example, even had to wait until the very last night of his last term before fulfilling the traditional dare for such a swell of taking a swim in the adjacent girls' school pool, for fear of immediate expulsion. Homosexuality then seemed to me to be an enforced problem that people just outgrew. Even more than a school, a small crowded ship must have been a difficult venue for such clandestine intimacies.

It used to be said that there were only three serious disciplinary problems in the Royal Navy, and they all revolved around 'rum, bum and "baccy" '. Ships' notice-boards would plead with the sailors not to smuggle duty-free tobacco ashore, on the grounds that the civilian population was already restless about this naval privilege. On the one hand it took the Admiralty many years of peacetime to pluck up the courage to withdraw the rum-ration from the ships; on the other hand, the second of the three problems had prompted an early and rather embarrassed Confidential

Admiralty Fleet Order, which offered commanding officers tentative legal and medical advice on that subject. All I can report is that, over the next two years in NARCISSUS, there was no indication that what I had witnessed had been more than a slightly bizarre and isolated occurrence. Perhaps I was too unworldly to recognize signs of emotional attachment; if there was any relevant wardroom gossip on the subject, I was certainly unaware of it.

Towards a freedom of information

There were lots of other sorts of gossip; rumours, or 'buzzes' as the Navy preferred to call them, within and between ranks. Wartime counter-propaganda brainwashed us all into mistrusting rumour as probably inspired by the enemy; this was often achieved most effectively and amusingly by the cartoonist Fougasse. The fact was, nevertheless, that many depressing rumours turned out to be true, even if only years later. The value of Fougasse and his work, one supposes, was that it cast enough doubt on bad news to give time for civilian morale to regain its balance. One example from civilian life was the rumour circulated, at a British community fete in Rio de Janeiro not long before I was due to leave, that two British battleships had just been sunk. It was dismissed as an attempt by the local German 'colony' to spoil the day for us but, unfortunately, it was true.

How did one get to know, aboard NARCISSUS, about ructions in ships of the convoy, about the fate of ships in other convoys and so on? News did not so much travel downwards from officers to ratings, as in the belief of at least one author,[1] as upwards from crew to officers. The signals officer and the Captain, in my experience anyway, used to maintain the smirk of the *cognoscenti* about all the coded signals, unaware that the ratings were keeping the rest of us abreast of the choicer gobbets of news.

We must have been indebted ultimately, for our special news items, to a benevolent wireless operator, coder or signalman. Information was not so much power, in this context, as its dissemination represented prestige. How could a communications rating resist the temptation of sharing a juicy slice of information with his 'winger' on the mess deck? For the officers, on the other hand, the proper source of signalled information should have been its exclusive recipient, the Captain; more often than not, however, someone like Leading Artificer Greene would give us the 'buzz'.

The Captain saves my deep embarrassment

It must have become clear to the persevering reader of these meanderings that the Captain is not being portrayed as a very sympathetic figure: indeed, he came over to me as a rather withdrawn person, apparently nursing some secret sorrow. One is now tempted to suspect that his professional pride was still smarting from his failure to find and succour the freighter SHANTUNG the previous year. I personally had no right, of course, to expect any particular warmth and, no doubt, my technical ignorance must often have tried his patience. And yet – I do recall one occasion when he supported me somewhat against the odds and certainly against the ire of the crew.

I had started to stand the middle watch on my own. One night was moonless but clear, with only the horizon lighted by a starlit sky. As we were zigzagging ahead of the convoy, I suddenly saw the hulls of several ships, right ahead and lifted against the horizon. I immediately thought we were running into another convoy. What I should have done was either to ask the Radar operator to give me a range, or glance at the binnacle to check the ship's heading. Instead, all I could recall was the Captain's standing order: 'If there is any danger to the ship or convoy, ring the alarm.'

So I whacked the alarm buzzer and, as figures started to emerge from below pulling on sweaters and boots, I then managed to look at the binnacle; only to discover the

NARCISSUS was now heading towards our own convoy instead of away from it. What had happened was that the quartermaster, in the wheelhouse on the deck below me, still had five degrees of starboard helm on, which had carried us way past the starboard leg of the zigzag. It was normal for an escort vessel to zigzag either side of the convoy course, the helmsman changing course automatically every ten minutes.[2] Unfortunately, the quartermaster had fallen asleep whilst changing course, his bos'n's mate was away getting cocoa for the watch and I had failed to notice that the ship had kept swinging to starboard.

As the gun captains, damage control party leaders, etc. had arrived on the bridge for orders, they had to be turned away with 'Sorry! False alarm!'. This was not popular, especially with the daymen. There was naturally much sucking of teeth, choking back of weary criticism and some not very inaudible insubordination. Particularly upset was the formidable Chief Bos'n's Mate; being a dayman without a night watch, he appreciated having his night disturbed only in a real emergency. Quite surprisingly the Captain, whose confirmation of the chorus of disapproval I cringingly awaited, silenced the red-headed giant with a sharp 'Quite right to sound the alarm in the circumstances!' On this occasion the only damage was to a night's sleep, but I later wondered if this error in zigzagging was what had happened in the tragic case of the cruiser CURACOA which, at about that same date, was run over with heavy loss of life when escorting the troopship RMS QUEEN MARY.

Illusion, hallucination and disillusion

Fatigue and the problems of night vision helped to create other illusions on the North Atlantic. A mysterious and as yet unexplained aftermath of one convoy battle involved a report by two Merchant Navy officers. They were from the British motor vessel JAMAICAN PRODUCER and were debriefed by an intelligence officer on arrival in Cardiff. The two reported that, '. . . at 2313 [hrs] on 10th March 1943 [in convoy HX228] a heavy explosion was heard on a Free French corvette which was steaming about two cables distant on the port beam forward. The corvette was torpedoed and her depth charge exploded.'[3] HX228 was a convoy in which B3 Group was heavily engaged, as we shall see, yet no such event had occurred: no corvette was lost or damaged, so how could such a graphic description be forthcoming, not just from one witness but two?

Hallucination would not have been uncommon in the special circumstances of stress in naval warfare. During my personal learning period in the latter half of 1942, NARCISSUS was rushed out of the base at Argentia to look for a burning tanker, whose crew had already been taken off. It was thought that the U-boat which had torpedoed it was still in its vicinity. On finding the tanker we were ordered by radio to circle it at high speed, throughout the night, awaiting the arrival of a tug at dawn. That night,

1942 officers; note duffle-coats and leather boots.

Officer of the watch, cowering between the magnetic and gyro compasses!

during my solitary middle watch, with a starlit moonless sky over a flat-calm sea, I began to see a rim of light marking the corvette's track around the faraway burning ship. Mesmerised like a chicken in a chalk circle, I then began to imagine that track as being the rim around the huge black void of a gigantic saucer. It took me several minutes to persuade myself that we were not about to fall over this vertiginous edge into a black chasm.

One final disillusion which I was to experience in this initial learning period related to preconceptions I had about personal hygiene. I had got used to sleeping in my clothes, of course, merely shedding duffle-coat, sou'wester and the heavy top-boots; the latter had to be snug enough to keep out sub-zero temperatures and, especially, loose enough not to drag down and drown the wearer if he were unfortunate enough to end up in the sea.

One item not shed in between watches became so close to my person that it has become the only contemporary kit that

I have kept ever since. At a recent Normandy Veterans' Association reunion, when members were asked to display mementos on a table, I was mildly miffed that this article was neither recognized nor excited comment. I refer, of course, to regulation issue North Atlantic Heavy Duty Underpants or, as they were known more affectionately, 'Bull's Wool Drawers'. If any one thing ever kept this sailor alive and hopeful, these heavily ribbed, machine-knitted, ankle-length 'comforts', made of virgin wool with the lanolin left in, were it; but the price lay in constant washing. It is almost beyond my belief now to learn that some corvetteers, based on Belfast, were prepared to 'flog' them to the dockyard mateys there![4]

There was but a single bathroom for the six (and later more) officers in a corvette; and this tiny space contained a real bath. The entirely sensible and more economical arrangement of a shower was too new-fangled for those days. Soon after my arrival in NARCISSUS I was told that, as the official solution to the extravagance of providing hot water for officers' baths, the same bathwater was to be taken in order of seniority. As the sole Sub-Lieutenant, mine would be the last turn.[5]

References

[1] J. Rusbridger, 1991, *Who Sank Surcouf?*, Century, p. 163: 'In the RN there is a great tradition of what is called 'buzz': news which circulates around the lower deck largely promulgated by wishful thinking and a few scraps of information obtained by those who may have overheard some conversation between officers.'

[2] There had been intermittent discussions about the duration and extent of zigzags, e.g. early in 1942 *vide* ADM 237/192. The breadth of the zigzag was determined by such factors as other ships nearby, the relative speeds of freighters and escorts, and the width of the screen to be provided; but the principal factor, obviously, was the distraction it offered to U-boat aim. Independently-sailing merchantmen zigzagged; for ships in convoy to be zigzagging, however, would have led to collisions without

necessarily gaining immunity and reassurance from the practice.
[3] ADM 199/1145; see also ADM 199/576.
[4] Chris Howard Bailey, (Ed.), 1994, *The Battle of the Atlantic*. The corvettes and the crews: an Oral History, Alan Sutton, p. 109.
[5] Here I must confess that my recent, incomplete trawl through the whole gamut of Admiralty Fleet Orders, from 1939 to 1942, has failed to turn up any such instruction from Their Lordships; I now think it likely that I was the victim of an elaborate wardroom jape. We always had the solace of a wash-basin and ewer in our cabins, of course; the water in the bath-tap was apparently salt water anyway (see Howard Bailey, p. 107). What puzzles me now is: why have I continued to think that the bath-water was expensive fresh water? Did I never get a bath until I went on leave?

Apart from published material and personal information, the following unpublished sources have been used in this chapter: ADM 182/127 (for CAFO 648/40); ADM 187/20; ADM 199/576, & 582, 583, 716, 1145, 1338, 1729.

CHAPTER 5

The Winter of 1942/43. The weather is an enemy as well

After the amalgamation of the old 3EG and 4EG into B3 Group in February 1942 on the Clyde, the old 'B' class destroyers had gone off northwards to start escorting convoys to Russia. One of the corvettes that BULLDOG had taken with her out of 3EG for the summer months was ROSELYS. She now returned to the Clyde and henceforth remained with her Free French sisters in B3.

On 16 November B3 Group met an old British submarine and its escort, which usually doubled up as a dummy target; at that rendezvous off the north coast of Ireland the Group practised warding off attacks upon the submarine's consort. Then HARVESTER, GARLAND, NARCISSUS, ORCHIS, LOBELIA, ROSELYS and ACONIT took up their task of shepherding the slow convoy ONS146 (Commodore HC Forsythe in ATHOL PRINCE) westwards. The path of the convoy led more southwards than usual at only 6½ knots and, on reaching the Western Ocean Meeting Point (WESTOMP) and in the apparent absence of the enemy, ACONIT and LOBELIA were permitted to proceed to the French island of St Pierre, off the southern coast of Newfoundland.

The next day a storm struck; that, together with an HF/DF bearing of a U-boat transmitting, delayed any further splitting of the convoy into its destination sections.

NARCISSUS was given the task of running out on the bearing and did in fact sight the conning-tower, but the state of the sea and the corvette's inferior speed put any realistic attack out of the question. The convoy was now not so much split as scattered by the storm anyway. A representative experience was that of the British freighter WALLSEND, which had no recourse but to head independently south-eastwards across the Atlantic towards her destination, Freetown. Off the Cape Verde Islands, however, she was torpedoed by a U-boat which surfaced, gave the survivors a compass bearing to the nearest land and carried off the ship's master as a prisoner.

HX218

After that ONS convoy, slightly disorientated though it was but at least undamaged whilst it was in our care, the Escort Group lay over in Newfoundland's two naval bases; the two destroyers and NARCISSUS docked in St John's and the other corvettes in the harbour at Argentia. Before noon on 10 December 1942 we left St John's with 11 ships for HX218 (Commodore, Admiral Sir Eric Fullerton, RN, Rtd.). In 25 hours we found the rest of the Group and convoy. This comprised 55 ships, half of which were tankers, hence the presence of an extra support unit consisting of two ex-American four-stackers, HMS GEORGETOWN and HMS LINCOLN (named, as usual, after towns common to both countries). This passage, although relatively rich in incident, was also mercifully free of enemy success. At 1400 hours on 13 December in 53°10'N 42°18'W, GARLAND rescued Henry Edward Hanson, Able Seaman, in a portion of Tank Landing Craft 312, which had floated off the upper deck of SS BARBARY when she was torpedoed on 26 November, seventeen days earlier. This spot in the ocean was roughly 600 miles equidistant from both the south of Greenland and the east coast of Canada. Was there ever a luckier Able Seaman?

At the same time HF/DF intercepts indicated the presence of U-boats astern, so the four destroyers swept back along the track of the convoy, but found nothing. Meanwhile the Commodore was asked to turn the whole convoy 30° to port at 1900 hours, to shake off any shadower, and then back again 40° to starboard four hours later.

The next day GARLAND sighted and narrowly missed ramming a U-boat; and a Liberator aircraft from Iceland attacked a U-boat 20 miles astern of the convoy. As a discouragement to any potential shadower, GARLAND was sent back that night to sweep astern on her own, whilst the convoy executed yet another 42° turn to starboard. Some comfort now seemed to be offered to the threatened ships by the arrival of three anti-submarine trawlers, but the Senior Officer of the escorts was not much impressed. He thought the trawlers too slow to keep up and, in their effort to do so, they tended to make too much smoke and thus give the position away.

Commander Tait was also irritated to find that, when he wanted one of the supporting destroyers to top up with fuel from an accompanying tanker, she was unable to do so because she did not carry the right adaptors to connect with any of the oil suppliers present. 1942 was a year of innovations in the Battle of the Atlantic, but it was also a year of teething troubles. Reinforcement by the two four-stackers foreshadowed the regular provision of stronger support groups which would then be able to hunt U-boats to extinction; this policy had only been established in September of that year. Similarly, refuelling escorts at sea had only started in June.[1] The full benefits of those innovations would take a year to mature. Although the passage of this convoy was otherwise uneventful, back at the land headquarters in Greenock, in his subsequent report on the lessons to be learned from it, Captain 'D' thought fit to rebuke the Captain of GARLAND for not puncturing a calcium flare, which had been jettisoned to mark his near-miss of a U-boat. Similarly, it was regretted that flashless cordite had not been at hand for the destroyer's 4.7-inch gun, so that the gun's crew need not have been blinded temporarily when they opened fire at night. As if in contrition, Captain 'D' did balance these strictures upon a gallant ally by praising LOBELIA's Asdic operator for his alertness in detecting a U-boat, which the corvette was then able to drive away from the convoy.

The day we arrived back in the Clyde was my twentieth birthday. Both NARCISSUS and ORCHIS were due for a boiler-clean, which would put them out of service for a week; so both ships were able to grant leave until 27 December. Of the officers it was only fair that the married men should spend Christmas at home and just the First Lieutenant and I were left on board. Hugh Meeke, with typical generosity, must have shared with me the burden of duty officer-of-the-watch, although he was under no obligation to do so; for I vaguely recollect spending the evening of that arrival in harbour, on 20 December, at the local watering-hole, the bar of the Bay Hotel, Gourock. This was the domain of a famous character, who was as broad as she was tall. If she favoured you, especially if you were Free French, she would permit her left aureole to be encircled with the tip of a forefinger. My only clear memory of that visit was an enthusiastically-applauded performance of this gentle ritual by a young officer, later to become a distinguished citizen; it was Christmas time after all.

Taken under the wing of some fellow Christmas-exiles from the destroyer BULLDOG, which happened to be in harbour, the self-plastering process proceeded in their ship. I found myself spending the night on their wardroom sofa and was lucky not to be carried out to sea with them the next day, probably towards Murmansk. Only much later did I discover the role BULLDOG had played in the Battle as a leader in the Clyde Escort Force.

ON157

HARVESTER was due for a refit, so she did not sail with us on our next convoy westwards. Either Commander Tait took rather seriously Captain 'D's remarks about GARLAND's inadequate procedures during her attack upon that U-boat, or he could not bring himself to take leave with the rest of his destroyer's crew. At any rate, he signalled that: 'GARLAND not qualified to command an escort group at present,' and embarked in her himself as Senior Officer.

HMS VIMY wad delegated as substitute destroyer, but eventually could not sail because of engine defects and the frigate SWALE came instead. Convoy ON157 of 40 ships (Commodore TH Owen, RNR, OBE in the Norwegian SKIENSFJORD) was middling fast, 7.5 knots average speed, and there was again little interference from the enemy.

With the sea getting rough at this time, some of the escorts found oiling difficult. Oil-hoses were being torn open in the then standard 'astern' method of refuelling escorts, who had to pursue in the wake of the oiler. In the later years of the Battle, all ships would adopt the 'alongside' method, which made it easier for the receiving ship's captain to stay level and to maintain his distance away from the tanker.

Soon after the ocean escorts left their charges at the customary WESTOMP southeast of Newfoundland, the Commodore reported the absence of one ship. She was a faster type of ship, capable of 11½ knots and, with the weather worsening, had probably decided to romp ahead.

On 8 January ROSELYS and ACONIT were permitted to go and enjoy a Gallic welcome at St Pierre, whereas poor LOBELIA had to make do with the delights of St John's, together with the rest of the ships of the Group.

Whilst we were in St John's in mid-January we heard on the grape-vine (probably from Canadians at the 'Buzzard's Crutch') an horrific account of the experiences of the ex-American ROXBOROUGH. Mention of her struck a chord, because she had formed part of the Clyde Escort Force the previous year. She was at that very moment limping back to harbour under the command of a young RCNVR Sub-Lieutenant.

Bad weather had been threatening before we ourselves had arrived in harbour. The same seas were now mountainous and, in them, ROXBOROUGH had been struck on the beam by two successive 60-foot-high waves. She rolled with the first, but stiffly so that, as she was coming upright again, she was struck by the second with the combined force, not only of the wave itself, but also of the returning impetus of the ship's roll. Our informants told us that the destroyer Captain had been in his sea-cabin; escort ships' captains often spent much of a difficult passage there, so as to be within seconds of reaching the bridge in an emergency. In this account the cabin's port-hole scuttle had been driven in by the weight of the sea, the cabin had filled with water and the Captain had drowned before he could get out of an accommodation space which normally might have been forty feet above sea-level.

To us this account was immediately believable as we had all been in beam seas in the North Atlantic when two ships, perhaps only 300 yards apart in parallel wave-troughs, could barely see each other at intervals. The captain's sea-cabin in a corvette, also, was half-way up the port side of the bridge and did not even have a port-hole, but a sash window with a wooden roller-blind.

Anyone seeking confirmation of this account would find Admiralty records which show that, on 15 January, GEORGETOWN (the same Town class destroyer which had, with LINCOLN, supported our December convoy) and ROXBOROUGH were returning to St John's after acting as support to convoy HX222 when they encountered very heavy weather: '. . . GEORGETOWN reported ROXBOROUGH's bridge carried away and requested the assistance of a tug and escort as she [GEORGETOWN] anticipated having to leave due to the fuel situation.' An inexplicit announcement of the death of the Captain of ROXBOROUGH (he had served in her since May 1942) also appears in the 'Obituaries' section of the Navy List for April 1943.

It is a nice calculation as to whether or not the Royal and the Royal Canadian Navies would have been better off without the 50 Town class destroyers with which the United States bought the use of British harbours on the east coast of the Americas. The Americans could have and probably would have, in the event of a British armistice, just taken possession of the harbours, for their own protection against German expansionism. On the credit side, bases like Argentia became very useful to us; perhaps we should have given them up freely, accepting only the services which they eventually provided. GEORGETOWN's signal, shown above, indicated a further one of the Town class's shortcomings which is not touched upon by Middlebrook in his summation below: that is their inability to stay at sea for more than a short period without refuelling. It was a failing that B3 Group was to regret very much in the following March, when two of them were the destroyer consorts of the first escort carrier to join the Atlantic Battle (apart, of course, from the short-lived HMS AUDACITY in the Bay of Biscay, referred to later).

Whilst the value of that class of destroyer as a whole may be debatable, what is not in doubt is the opinion of those who had the misfortune to serve in them: 'Their crews hated them. They were narrow ships which rolled viciously; their propellor shafts stuck out several feet beyond the stern and they were very difficult to handle. They had a huge turning circle which was not much help when attacking a U-boat. They were certainly unsuited to Atlantic weather: at least two had their bridges smashed by heavy seas and in one of these the captain and several others were crushed and killed.'[2]

The US Navy must have been glad to see the back of those fifty. In August 1944 the Royal Navy passed ROXBOROUGH on to the Soviet Navy, where she became the DOBLESTNI.

SC117

Four days after ROXBOROUGH's disaster, B3 Group left St John's and headed straight into the blizzard. The Senior Officer had now transferred himself to SWALE. The next day the convoy became scattered and all the escorts were in trouble with snow and frozen sea-spray on the forecastles. Whenever it was safe to do so, the duty watch was turned to with axes and hot water hoses to chip and melt away the ice which had threatened to overcome even the renowned buoyancy of the whaler-shaped corvettes. Nevertheless LOBELIA developed a dangerous list to port and the ice rendered her depth-charge throwers inoperative, so that by 23 January she had to return to St John's. This, in itself, is some indication of how much headway had *not* been achieved in four days against the storm.

HMS WITCH had sailed to join us, but returned to St John's within three days with her foremast carried away. Even by 20 January it had been every ship for herself, the climate having made systematic warfare impossible for either side. Convoy SC117 (40 ships, Commodore H. Woodward, RNR, in GEISHA) never really recovered its composure: although sufficient control had been established by the 27th, two casualties, SS LACKENBY and SS MOUNT MYCALE, remained unaccounted for, even when the remainder arrived in port on 3 February.

Stories went the rounds (probably passed on by the radio operators, who were listening in to plain language chatter on the Radio/Telephone) of ships overturning when top-heavy with ice: one message retailed with bated breath was that a Commodore's ship had so perished, but it was hardly policy to dwell on such misfortunes.

Only recently could it be confirmed that, on 21 January 1943, the former French vessel VILLE DE TAMATAVE, carrying the Commodore of convoy ONS160, Vice-Admiral Sir Henry Brownrigg, RN (Rtd.), '. . . turned over in storm-force winds; all hands were lost.'[3] This was almost certainly the catastrophe which was relayed to us over the grapevine;

convoy ONS160 would have been heading into the storm at the same time as we were running before it.

Vice-Admiral Brownrigg is said to have been the highest-ranking officer to have been lost on either side during the War; no fewer than 21 very senior officers, most of them retired admirals, gave their lives serving as Commodores RNR during the Battle.

In the middle of all this the C-in-C Western Approaches ordered an evasive turn northwards but Commander Tait, whether from other information or from a disinclination to make matters worse, exercising his rights as the man on the spot, tactfully declined to do so and signalled back that 'owing to HF/DF [bearings of U-boat signals] it was undesirable to alter [the course of the convoy]'.

The C-in-C tried again on the 28th to bring the convoy closer to the outer limits of air cover, but Tait replied that the convoy was running before a westerly gale and that he intended to continue on the present course until the weather moderated. Nobody with the convoy thought that the U-boats would be doing anything more dangerous than keeping their heads down – probably about 200 feet down!

FS LOBELIA distinguishes herself

In the meantime our LOBELIA fell on her feet. It will be remembered that she had had to return to St John's, having been incapacitated by ice; when thawed out, she was loaned to the next convoy escort to come eastwards; this was B2 Group escorting SC118 of 61 ships.

Normally that Group was commanded by the very experienced and successful Commander Donald Macintyre, but he had unfortunately been taken ill and his temporary replacement spread the escort ships inappropriately around the convoy (I merely repeat the opinion expressed in the biography of Gilbert Roberts, the tactical 'guru' of Western Approaches Command).[4]

Captain Roberts taught that U-boats, when attacking at

night, should be expected to come from upwind and the prevailing wind in the North Atlantic was from the west. The bulk of the escorts of SC118 was disposed ahead of the easterly-bound convoy; only LOBELIA kept the rescue ship TOWARD company, as a rearguard. On 4 February the large and apparently expected target of 61 ships was sighted by the middle boat of the PFEIL wolf-pack assembled by Dönitz. Altogether 20 U-boats[5] were brought up, of which several found their way into SC118 from astern.

The PFEIL group sank 10 merchantmen, including the rescue ship. Roberts's biographer gives a sympathetic account of LOBELIA's heroic struggle against these odds and she was credited with sinking U-609. Out of contact with her leader, due to an imposed R/T and W/T silence, LOBELIA warded off one boat after another all night and expended 180 depth-charges. Her exploits were soon to be overshadowed by those of her compatriot ACONIT, but we were all very proud that she had given such a good account of herself.

ON(S)167

This outward-bound convoy was small, slow and ultimately wearisome: 28 ships (including three oilers and the rescue ship RATHLIN) under Captain IW Whitehorn RN (Rtd.), serving as a Commodore RNR, was billed at 6.5 knots and eventually achieved an average of 5.7 knots. Even so, two ships were sent back to Liverpool as being unable to keep up; this is some indication of how many old tubs were being pressed into service at this stage of the War.

Paradoxically, the escort was stronger than usual: HARVESTER was back with us, together with ESCAPADE and two of our Polish friends, BURZA and GARLAND; of the corvettes ACONIT, ROSELYS and RENONCULE accompanied NARCISSUS. Even before reaching the longitude deemed unsafe for unescorted ships, i.e. 8°West, our westbound group of merchantmen was already scattered by the mid-February gale; their steerage was not helped by being mostly in ballast of course. We were soon gratified to hear ESCAPADE signal over the airwaves to the Senior Officer: 'NARCISSUS and 12 ships in sight.'

The Admiralty had frequently been able to warn convoy escorts of U-boat patrol lines and concentrations, using the probable euphemism of 'HF/DF bearings', which were really Ultra decrypts of Enigma code signals from U-boats. The position of a single U-boat on passage to its patrol area, however, would always be unpredictable until it signalled its arrival to Dönitz. So it was just fortuitous, nearly a week later on the night of 21 February, when the outward-bound U-664 came across ONS167 and managed to sink the American ROSARIO and the Panamanian HH ROGERS. RATHLIN succeeded in picking up 30 survivors out of the ROSARIO's crew of 63 as well as 66 from the HH ROGERS, including the whole of the US Navy Guard on board, numbering 26. NARCISSUS also picked up 7 Americans.

The next day BURZA sighted two U-boats on the surface and drove them off. Despite these threats, no further losses occurred and on the 26th the escorts started to disperse as the local relief group took over: HARVESTER to St John's for repairs; GARLAND to land a serious burns cot-case; and NARCISSUS to escort the freighter SUERTE to St John's and to land the American survivors. RATHLIN continued with the convoy and did not land her survivors until 6 March, at Halifax.[6]

In March 1943 the numbering of Outward-bound, North, (Slow) convoys was changed: slow ones were now numbered consecutively on their own starting again. Thus, whereas we had escorted ON(S)167 in February, we would escort ONS18 the following September.

March 1943, the crisis month

The gales and rising temperatures of the northern Spring were now causing the break-up of the Arctic fringe; from now on maverick icebergs would float across the mouth of St John's harbour in Newfoundland. Warships might now need to cut through a foot-thick veneer of ice-pancake floes before they could even start their escorting duties.

This was the climatic environment in which one particularly critical convoy battle was fought; a battle which represented a low point of British fortunes. This dark event was the struggle for the fast convoy HX229 which became, for the Germans at least, indistinguishable from the attack on the adjacent convoy SC122; these two convoys were under the care of B4 and B5 Ocean Escort Groups respectively. Neither one was escorted by B3 Group, but they are mentioned here because their experience helps to outline the context within which B3 had fought a battle only one week earlier.

Apart from the frequency with which HX229 and SC122 are referred to in naval histories, these two convoys have had a particular fascination for British writers: for example, they have become central topics in Middlebrook's 1976 documentary, *Convoy*, and in Harris's 1995 novel, *Enigma*.

Contemporary German accounts of the attack upon HX229/SC122 were ecstatic and exaggerated: '. . . the largest and most successful action in the U-boat war to date . . . our U-boats sank 32 ships (totalling 204,000 gross tons) of this convoy and one destroyer.'[7]

Subsequent British historians were more accurate and more dour: 'No battle fought at sea during the Second World War had to contend with such difficulties . . . During a 3-day battle, 23 merchantmen were sunk . . . only one submarine sunk.'[8]

Perhaps most relevant to our own story is one summary of the weather damage: 'The storms of that appalling March helped to do Dönitz's work, for another 10 ships of HX229 and SC122 either foundered or had to put back to port.'[9]

One of today's leading military historians includes the March convoy battles among the 'Fifteen Decisive Sea Battles' of all human history.[10] It was in this same apocalyptic month that B3 Group experienced its own crises of sacrifice and triumph, escorting the preceding eastbound convoy: HX228.

References

[1] Correlli Barnett, 1991, *Engage the Enemy More Closely*, Hodder & Stoughton, p. 481.

[2] Martin Middlebrook, 1978, *Convoy*, Penguin, p. 32.

[3] John Slader, 1994, *The Fourth Service. Merchantmen at War, 1939–1945*, Robert Hale, p. 295.

[4] Mark Williams, 1979, *Captain Gilbert Roberts RN and the Anti-Uboat School*, Cassell, pp. 121–2.

[5] J. Rohwer & G. Hummelchen, 1974, *Chronology of the War at Sea, 1939–1945*, Vol. II, The Military Book Society, pp. 296–7.

[6] see Rohwer & Hummelchen, Vol. II, p. 304 for the identity of U-664 only (i.e. not of the escort group!).

[7] Janusz Piekalkiewicz, 1987, *Sea War 1939–1945*, (Trans. by Peter Spurgeon), p. 248.

[8] Slader, *op. cit.*, p. 152.

[9] Barnett, *op. cit.*, p. 599.

[10] John Keegan, 1993, *A History of Warfare*, Hutchinson, pp. 67–8.

The unpublished sources used in this chapter are: ADM 177/45; ADM 187/20, & 22; ADM 199/71, & 579, 583, 1705, 2101; ADM 237/130, & 663.

Forecastle, covered in frozen spray.

Pancake ice on the open sea, 1942/43.

Port side forward, covered in snow.

Amidships, covered in snow.

*Forepart of NARCISSUS,
taken from the crow's-nest.*

*Afterpart of
NARCISSUS, taken
from the crow's-nest.*

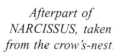

CHAPTER 6

HX228 – The Lost Leader

HX228 was an inward-bound, fast convoy of 60 ships in 13 columns, 3 to 5 rows deep (Commodore J. O. Dunn, RNR, in SS TETELA). Normally, the centre columns were intended to harbour the valuable cargoes, troops, oil and ammunition. The Germans probably knew this, for they frequently attempted to enter the centre columns from ahead at night. In HX228, a space was left in the middle for one of the new escort aircraft-carriers. These freighters were converted to carry a flight deck and were intended to bridge the mid-Atlantic gap between cover from Canadian aircraft and from other Allied aircraft based in Iceland and Scotland.

The Naval Escorts

The ocean escort was provided by B3 Group, led by HMS HARVESTER, under the command of Commander A. A. Tait RN, DSO, the Senior Officer. HMS ESCAPADE, another British destroyer, now joined the Group on a regular basis. Also present were the British corvette HMS NARCISSUS, two Polish destroyers ORP GARLAND and ORP BURZA, and three Free French units, the corvettes FFS ACONIT FFS RENONCULE and FFS ROSELYS. Despite the absence of two regular members, HMS ORCHIS and FFS LOBELIA, on duty elsewhere, the presence of four destroyers made this a more formidable close escort than had been customary until this phase of the Battle.

The protection of the merchant ships was taken over from the local escort force at the usual meeting point south of Newfoundland on the morning of the 6th March, 1943. That same afternoon the 6th Escort Group arrived, comprising the American escort carrier USS BOGUE protected by two old, modified, four-funnelled destroyers. Thus was repeated that innovative enterprise of December 1941, convoy HG76, but which had ended with the loss of the escort carrier HMS AUDACITY. The idea was the same: an aggregation of urgently-needed war supplies should cross to Britain with, not only surface protection, but also taking its own aerial reconnaissance and strike power. In HX228 in March 1943, the carrier BOGUE took up her station between the 5th and sixth columns and the two destroyers were allocated a place in the peripheral escort screen.

Ultra decrypts just fail to avert contact with the enemy

The convoy then sailed on eastwards into the mid-Atlantic. As it approached the eastern half of the ocean, Commander Tait recommended to the Commodore a radical turn to starboard. Many of us in the escort ships who were not privy to the real source of the information available to our Senior Officer thought that some of his sudden alterations of convoy course were inspired to the point of genius. Several times during the previous winter we had received signals implying the looming danger of wolf-packs, only for him, at the last moment, to order a 45 degree turn to port or starboard which carried us all away from the threat.

Because of the direction-finding equipment on board, we knew that the compass-bearing and distance away of individual U-boats could be gauged from the signals they were transmitting to Dönitz. Indeed Hinsley has now disclosed that the term 'direction finding' was a euphemism for Enigma, the German coding system[1]; but we had no idea that the Code and Cypher School at Bletchley Park was actually decrypting those signals on behalf of the Admiralty.

Presumably Commander Tait did not know where this miraculous information was coming from either, in view of the 'Ultra' secrecy surrounding it, but he always made good use of the 'advice' which reached him over the air-waves.

Unfortunately, the German decoding service, *B-Dienst*, also decoded and passed on the new course given to HX228[2] as it drew level with a line of 18 U-boats, whose nucleus was the wolf-pack '*NEULAND*'. At midday on 10th March U-336, the southernmost in the North/South line, sighted the flock of ships and called down the remainder of the pack upon the fold.[3] No fault can be found with the evasive turn taken by the convoy. This tactic was usually employed at dusk and was dangerous in itself: one out of sixty-odd ships might well either miss the order and find itself steaming along alone next morning, or turn too far and run into its neighbour. Too big a turn might merely send the convoy into a different awaiting ambush: there were at least three other wolf-packs in the North Atlantic that night.

Attack by NEULAND Group, night of 10/11 March 1943

As the light fades, HARVESTER orders the eight escort ships to night screening stations: NARCISSUS to a position in front of the centre column of merchant ships; a destroyer on the forward wing either side of the convoy; HARVESTER abreast the last ship on the starboard wing and BURZA in the equivalent position on the port side; and the three Free French corvettes across the back, RENONCULE to port, ACONIT to starboard and ROSELYS at 'longstop', in a position normally occupied by a specialist rescue ship. The positioning is significant for later events: HARVESTER is initially in a position to con the coming battle and, when she will call for assistance from far behind the starboard wing, it will be ACONIT who will be the nearest to her.

That night six ships in the centre and towards the starboard wing of the convoy are torpedoed; one catches fire and then blows up with a flash which lights up the ocean.

Later casualties are the Norwegian ammunition ship, SS BRANT COUNTY [no. 135, i.e. last ship in the 13th column], which blows up so violently, towards dawn, that she damages her killer, U-757; the exploding ammunition spreads high in the sky like a giant fan for all to see; also the Americans LAWTON EVANS [65] and WILLIAM G. GORGAS [131]. NARCISSUS picks up two survivors from the latter. In his report the Commodore will add that the SS JAMAICAN PRODUCER, mentioned in chapter 4, is also damaged by an 'internal explosion'.[4]

One account of how the battle developed comes from the captain of the corvette ACONIT himself. On the evening of the 10th March, Commander Tait tells ACONIT to take station at the back of the convoy and Lieutenant Levasseur is pleased, on account of the 'panoramic' view of any action to be gained from that position and for the opportunity it offers to waylay a U-boat after an attack.

At dusk there is an enormous explosion a mile ahead of ACONIT. On the bridge Levasseur looks quickly at his manifest of cargo locations; he notes that ships in column 7 are carrying ammunition and, indeed, the leading ship of that column, SS TUCURINGA [71], has been sunk and the ANDREW F. LUCKENBACK [74] has blown up. ACONIT gets an underwater contact and carries out a shallow attack with depth-charges. After her Asdic loses contact, Levasseur observes small red lights, those carried on the life-jackets of survivors, in the icy and oil-covered water; despite the normal rule that 'When an attack is in progress, the defence of the convoy takes precedence over the rescue of survivors', he spends a short while picking up the ones around him. One American sailor in an inflated rubber suit, looking rather like the Michelin advertisement, is covered in oil and cannot be hoisted on board, until one astute Frenchman punctures his suit with a knife!

U-444 had been one of the successful attackers, but was now surprised on the surface by the Senior Officer's destroyer, HARVESTER, who rams the U-boat abaft the conning-tower at a speed of 27 knots at 0100 hours in the morning. This deliberate collision is sufficient to prevent the German from submerging again but, unfortunately, it also disables the British ship. She overrides the submarine, which becomes jammed under her stern; meanwhile some of the U-boat's crew abandon ship and one survivor actually climbs aboard the destroyer.

The two crippled vessels draw apart and HARVESTER summons ACONIT to cover her whilst she tries to make good the damage. One of HARVESTER's two screw shafts is irreparably broken; she prepares to limp home on her remaining propellor. In the meantime, ACONIT has come across U-444, also in a distinctly vulnerable condition. The U-boat now gets rammed by the corvette and this time the blow is fatal only to the submarine. The Senior Officer orders ACONIT back to the still threatened convoy, which has been out of sight for a long time.

Before she leaves, however, ACONIT licks her wounds: the ramming has flooded the forward peak and the anchor chain locker, but the forward bulkheads hold out and the Asdic compartment is unharmed. Shouts in a strange language are heard from the water. A French sub-lieutenant exclaims: 'The skunks [les s . . . . . .], they are up the creek [patouille?] and they still call upon Hitler! Let them die!' Levasseur patiently explains that, far from calling upon the Führer, the U-boat survivors are uttering calls for help in German: 'Hilfe! Hilfe!' The Frenchmen pick up 5 Germans from U-444. A signal comes from HARVESTER: 'Well played!' One of the French crew, but born in the Sarre district, tells Levasseur that the first German whom he pulled out of the water was a class-mate from Sarrebruck.[5]

The sinking of HARVESTER

Her own misfortunes did not, however, prevent HARVESTER from continuing with her duty, as her captain saw it: hobbling after the convoy, she came across survivors from the American WILLIAM C. GORGAS, the previously leading ship of the starboard wing, and picked up 51 of them. At this juncture the remaining propellor shaft broke down and the Senior Officer sent for NARCISSUS and, again, ACONIT to stand by their leader. Ill-luck was handed out evenly that day: U-432, coming up from behind the convoy, observed the stationary destroyer and torpedoed her towards midday on the 12th; but ACONIT, returning to the scene of her previous success at full speed, detected the U-boat underwater with her Asdic set, forced it to the surface with depth-charges and despatched it with gunfire; the whole action taking just 23 minutes.[6]

ACONIT now proceeds to rescue HARVESTER's survivors. Whilst she is doing so a boatload of men from a ship in the port-wing column, the HENRY WYNKOOP (not a casualty of the night!), comes alongside.[7] Levasseur is tactfully silent about this incident, which is recorded by a fellow-Captain, de Morsier. The latter also makes known the bravery of the Captain of the WILLIAM C. GORGAS, who had been picked up earlier by HARVESTER. After the second sinking he refused the chance of a place on a raft, giving it up to a sailor and subsequently perished in the water. Levasseur rightly emphasizes the danger inherent in stopping to rescue, even the enemy, giving the example of the corvette HMS GLADIOLUS, whose last message before being torpedoed by U-558 in the North Atlantic in October 1941 had been: 'I am stopped and picking up survivors'.[8]

ACONIT's achievement in sinking two U-boats within twelve hours was unprecedented and, as far as I know, unmatched by any other corvette during the War. Magnificent though this undoubtedly was, perfection in the affairs of men is difficult to attain; the hard choice Levasseur now had to make subsequently drew some bitter comment from, in the first place, a survivor from HARVESTER and, later, from the Captain 'D' in the Group's home base of Greenock. ACONIT's own report showed that half an hour was devoted to picking up 20 German survivors from U-432, including the First Lieutenant. It is now part of Free French naval folklore that when one German reached for the scrambling net and realized that he was about to be rescued by Frenchmen, he preferred to push away again and drown.[9]

When a surviving officer of HARVESTER came to write his account of the tragedy on the 14th March, however, he had to point out that, between the ACONIT being sighted by the men in the water and their being rescued, very many died of exposure. 'In the case of one raft . . . out of 22 men only 2 were picked up.'[10] Captain Leslie Saunders RN, back in HMS ORLANDO, the so-called 'stone frigate' or shore-side administrative base for the escorts in Greenock, thought fit to repeat the implication that ACONIT should have proceeded to uplift the survivors of HARVESTER (and, of course, of GORGAS) before those of U-432.

Choices made between difficult options rarely please everybody and there are military grounds for putting the humanitarian option second: more than once in the War, the rescuing of casualties awaited the conclusion of the action; frequently the gathering of intelligence, or even the supply of misinformation, costs lives. On this occasion, Lieutenant Jean Levasseur may well have judged that the collection of information about that U-boat and about German perspectives at that crucial stage of the three-year Battle was more important. It was a sunny day and the seas not too rough. He had heard the Radio/Telephone summons to NARCISSUS and perhaps he thought she would get to HARVESTER's people first. Unfortunately NARCISSUS, coming over the opposite horizon and from much further away, did not arrive until two hours later.

The tally of survivors

Among those who were eventually picked up by ACONIT was the sole survivor from U-444. Some confusion was caused by his denial during interrogation that HARVESTER had ever rammed U-444, so that, for a while, it was thought that a third U-boat had been involved![11]

In the event ACONIT retrieved 29 survivors from HAR-VESTER, 25 Americans ex-GORGAS and 25 U-boat men that March afternoon in the North Atlantic. In his report three days later Lieutenant Briggs RNVR, the senior surviving officer, took particular care to praise highly the many men in the water. One instance of mutual encouragement was the singing of such currently popular bar-room songs as, 'Roll out the Barrel!' and 'You are my sunshine'. Because ACONIT had no medical officer, the Polish destroyer BURZA gallantly transferred her's by Carley float to care for the wounded. Even so, ACONIT had to bury an American and a German on successive nights.

It had been NARCISSUS's melancholy duty all through that climactic Winter and Spring of 1942/43 to pull merchant seamen from the water, Dutchmen, Norwegians and Americans as well as British. Many had been in a parlous state; not before had we had to recover people who were not only Royal Naval personnel, but also comrades-in-arms well known to us from frequent contact in the various ports.

Human beings who have been floating, or even sitting, in the freezing cold for four or five hours cannot be expected to be sprightly or even co-ordinated. Rescuing sailors would normally expect to have to go down their ship's side to haul the semi-comatose bodies up the scrambling nets. Yet, my own enduring memory, on that dispiriting occasion in March 1943 after the sinking of HARVESTER, was of a Carley-float (in those days an oblong tubular raft about two feet high, with a rope net for a floor), in which were sitting around the tube, facing inwards, eight or ten Chief and Petty Officers of the Royal Navy. They were not slumped in the characteristic attitudes of exhaustion, their caps were on at the regulation angle and they made no sound. As the float bumped alongside the corvette, each man got stiffly up in turn and attempted to climb the net. Naturally there was instant assistance from the waiting crew, but the example of fortitude was wasted on none present and I, for one, have never subsequently been able to observe a Royal Navy Petty Officer without remembering the calibre of those forebears.

Of the 34 survivors picked up by NARCISSUS, two died and were buried at sea that same night. The procedure for the final act is perhaps well known: each body in its own weighted canvas bag lies on an inclining plank; after a relatively perfunctory prayer offered by the ship's captain, the inboard end of the plank is lifted and the body is committed to the ocean.

Less well-known are the Navy's customary arrangements between the pronouncement of death and the burial. Apart from such purely administrative measures such as removal of an identification disc and personal effects for transmission to relatives, the principal task is to sew the body into the canvas. This distressing work cannot be left to just anyone. The isolation of an ocean-going community creates secondary occupations for those who are primarily sailors: every large ship has, for instance, its off-duty barber and tailor.

NARCISSUS did have a full-time Sick-Berth Attendant, but, happily, no full-time undertaker. So this duty was performed in March 1943 by a fairly gnarled, '3-badged' Able Seaman (the 3 golden chevrons on his arm signified 13 years Good Conduct – or, as Navy lore was more likely to suggest self-mockingly, 13 years of 'undetected crime'!). The task of sewing up the canvas merited the award of an undiluted tot of Navy rum per canvas. Tradition dictated further that the last stroke of the canvas needle should pass through the nasal septum of the remains. This was undoubtedly reassuring to the living, who might otherwise fear being consigned to the deep when merely dazed.

Among the survivors from HARVESTER, picked up by NARCISSUS, was a Canadian, Lieutenant Derek Lukin-Johnston RCNVR, who had sportingly left a shoreside appointment in order to gain some sea-going experience; one assumes that that was not the kind of experience he was seeking.

The aftermath

One of the Free French ships had been able to pick up 81 survivors from one of the stricken merchant ships, SS TUCURINGA, including 10 RAF passengers; but the next day the French captain had an unusual and slightly bizarre saga to recount. The leading ship of the port column, SS HENRY WYNKOOP, was undamaged but no longer had any lifeboats: when a tanker had blown up during the previous night, 18 men promptly abandoned the WYNKOOP. ROSELYS found them behind the convoy and took them back to their ship![12]

The loss of HARVESTER did not merely take away from us a friendly and distinguished Senior Officer – he was last seen swimming in the water with his cap on and his favourite pipe clenched in his teeth – but also it took most of his talented specialists. With them went the Irish surgeon, who taught us to sing 'Macnamara's Band' around the wardroom piano and other less mentionable ditties; together with the destroyer's only midshipman. Never again at parties would we sing that Western Approaches adaptation of 'The Twelve days of Christmas', when 'lords-a-leaping', 'five gold rings', 'partridges' etc. were replaced by 'destroyers hunting', 'U-boats diving', 'five Bloehm and Voss' and so on. That all now seemed rather too insouciant and First-World-Warish.

Also drowned with Commander Tait was his old friend, Commander G. G. Thompson, OBE, RN, who was taking passage home from Washington. He had the misfortune to displace a very lucky man: during three years of war, a Lieutenant Boyer RN had served in no less than five Allied submarines and destroyers which sank after he left them, including the French SURCOUF, referred to earlier. Boyer was also said to have commanded HMS ROXBOROUGH, but obviously not during the January 1943 storm, also referred to. In March he had been moved from HARVESTER to a sofa in ESCAPADE – and survived.[13]

B3 Group was not the only Escort Group to lose its leader,

because B7, a Londonderry-based escort group, lost FIREDRAKE on 16 December 1943 and B1 lost HURRICANE on Christmas Eve 1943; but, as a consequence of HARVESTER's loss, ramming was frowned upon as a method of despatching U-boats thereafter. So HX228's clash with *Gruppe* NEULAND had been short and bitterly sharp but not entirely unsatisfactory: the exchange of 5 merchant ships and a destroyer for 2 U-boats sunk and one heavily damaged was more profitable than that of the next HX convoy along, which was a real catastrophe; more importantly, many of the Allied crews were saved, whereas the Germans lost theirs to the sea or to prisoner-of-war camps.

One disappointment had been the inactivity of the escort carrier, which was supposed to make such a difference to the air cover afforded to the convoy. In order to fly off aircraft, the carrier had, of course, to head into the wind and this would usually mean having to move out of the convoy. BOGUE had operated anti-submarine patrols three days before the action took place. When the convoy was 900 miles west of Ireland on the morning of 10 March, the Senior Officer had asked for a further patrol to put down a signalling U-boat, 25 miles to the north. Two patrols went out, but both failed due to the breakdown of their depth-charge mechanisms.

Rohwer and Hümmelchen are tactful in their comments: 'The deployment of the BOGUE cannot be used to full advantage because the carrier sails in the middle of the convoy and has no freedom to manoeuvre.'[14] Captain (D) back in Greenock, perhaps stung by the loss of his old friend 'Harry' Tait, was more scathing: BOGUE was an embarrassment . . . an attraction to U-boats . . . report from RENONCULE [that] the American destroyers were continually talking on R/T and the escorting destroyers . . . made frequent approaches and flashed the challenge.'[15]

Official records place the carrier and her destroyers with HX228 until the 14th, but B3 Group members were disappointed to see her disappear just before the main U-boat attack began and this memory is supported by one account which states that: 'At 4 p.m. [on the 10th] the carrier and her escorts left the convoy to return to base.'[16] Perhaps it was feared that a concerted attack on the carrier had been ordered; after all, the first attack was, indeed, made through the middle of the convoy. Perhaps someone also remembered what had happened to HMS AUDACITY in 1941. At any event, 'the carrier remained most of the time in the convoy on account of the great U-boat danger and so had little freedom of movement for launching and landing of aircraft.'[17]

Sensing a potentially dangerous rift in inter-allied relations, the Commander-in-Chief, Western Approaches, eventually added his gloss to the more or less informed comments on the escort carrier's movements: 'It is unfortunate that the endurance of the destroyers escorting USS BOGUE necessitated the withdrawal of this vessel at such an important stage when the convoy was first threatened.'[18] This, of course, is further evidence of the unsuitability of those 'Town' class destroyers transferred to the Royal Navy for service in the North Atlantic: BOGUE's escorts were two of their sister ships which had not been transferred.

A curious historiographical postscript to the ineffectual presence of BOGUE is the published account that: 'The promised American support group [of BOGUE + escorts] did not go to sea with a convoy until the second half of March.'[19] Whereas, in fact, she was with HX228 as early as 6 March. Perhaps she was indulging in what the Navy calls a 'dry run': going through the motions of intervention in the Battle without yet being ready to fight. In which case, it probably was sensible to withdraw before too great expectations were aroused, despite the embarrassment only partly assuaged by the diplomacy of the Commander-in-Chief.

HX228 was not a turning point in the Battle: there was, after all, the disaster of HX229 still to come. For B3 Group, however, the nature of the contest did change and was

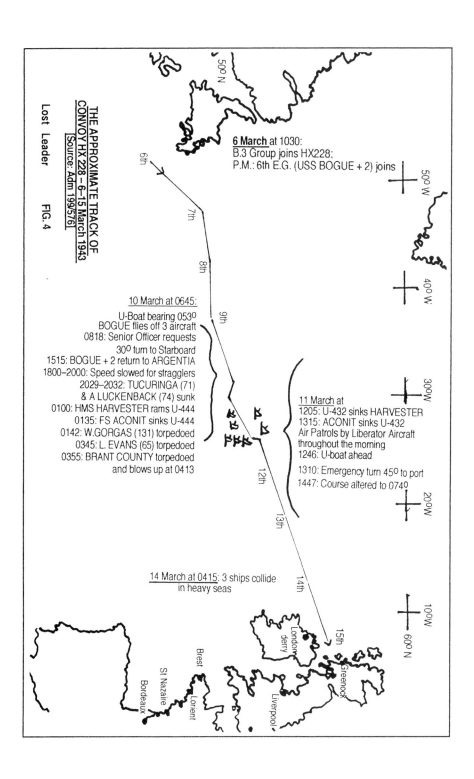

THE APPROXIMATE TRACK OF
CONVOY HX 228 – 6–15 March 1943
[Source: Adm 199/576]

Lost Leader   FIG. 4

6 March at 1030:
B.3 Group joins HX228;
P.M.: 6th E.G. (USS BOGUE + 2) joins

50° N

50° W

40° W

30°W

20°W

10°W

60° N

6th

7th

8th

9th

10 March at 0645:
U-Boat bearing 053°
BOGUE flies off 3 aircraft
0818: Senior Officer requests
30° turn to Starboard
1515: BOGUE + 2 return to ARGENTIA
1800–2000: Speed slowed for stragglers
2029–2032: TUCURINGA (71)
& A LUCKENBACK (74) sunk
0100: HMS HARVESTER rams U-444
0135: FS ACONIT sinks U-444
0142: W.GORGAS (131) torpedoed
0345: L. EVANS (65) torpedoed
0355: BRANT COUNTY torpedoed
and blows up at 0413

11 March at
1205: U-432 sinks HARVESTER
1315: ACONIT sinks U-432
Air Patrols by Liberator Aircraft
throughout the morning
1246: U-boat ahead

1310: Emergency turn 45° to port
1447: Course altered to 074°

12th

13th

14th

15th

14 March at 0415: 3 ships collide
in heavy seas

Londonderry
Greenock
Liverpool
Brest
St Nazaire
Lorient
Bordeaux

somehow reflected in the characters of the Senior Officers: before March 1943 the spirit of the Group seemed nonchalant and cavalier; after then there was a steely determination and a hardening professionalism. This was particularly noticeable in the Free French who were clearly inspired by the unique success of ACONIT. To borrow from Churchill, this was not the beginning of the end but the end of our beginning.

Tragically for HARVESTER, it was only after this battle that the strategy for the ultimate defeat of the U-boats began to fall into place: the last line of defence of the convoys continued to consist of the close screen of frigates and corvettes; *threatened* convoys, on the other hand, would get additional support from an extended screen of hunter-killers, which would now be able to stay with a detected U-boat until its extinction. The air-gap in mid-Atlantic could now be closed, either by MAC ships which stayed with the convoy throughout, or by Royal Naval carriers, organized into another form of Support Group, which could also move from convoy to convoy in mid-Ocean.

Long after the War, the National Maritime Museum at Greenwich wanted to illustrate a typical convoy battle of WWII and created a *'son et lumiere'*-type tableau, upon which were re-enacted all phases of a night encounter. The ship-models on the table were given the names of actual warships, principally the ships of B3 Escort Group and of the WILD GOOSE-class sloops of the 2nd Support Group. An outline of that exhibit is given at Figure 5. Unhappily for verisimilitude, this could not have been an historical convoy because, for example, HMS STARLING was not completed by her builders, Fairfields, until April 1943, whereas HMS HARVESTER, as we know, had already been sunk by U-432 on 11 March 1943. What the exhibit did demonstrate, however, was an idealized convoy defended by most of the contributors to the Battle of the Atlantic including Canadians (SKEENA), Norwegians (PONTENTILLA), Poles (GARLAND) and of course the French and British of the two Groups.

The air-contribution is well represented by the MACship, which has dropped out of the sixth column to fly off two Swordfish; and by a land-based Liberator, which is illuminating a U-boat ahead of the convoy. Also behind the convoy are a trawler, escorting the MACship and a firm friend of B3 Group's, the rescue ship ZAMALEK, attending a wounded freighter. The merchantmen are all numbered with their convoy positions and have already been infiltrated by at least two of the 15 U-boats on the surface.

Until this defensive pattern of two concentric screens could be kept in place continuously, a pause ensued in the summer of 1943 which was not unlike the period of 'slack water' between the ebb of the enemy tide and the flood of convoying success. For four months the U-boats were withdrawn to re-train and re-arm with secret and, they hoped, decisive weapons. But these months were not to be wasted by the Allies: by the time of the Germans' return to the North Atlantic, the new support system would be firmly in place.

German U-boat shelters in La Pallice today.

References

[1] Hinsley, F. H., 1981, *British Intelligence in the Second World War*, Vol. 2, HMSO p. 563. Nevertheless, it is worthwhile remarking that a U-boat captain who survived the War (Peter Cremer, *U333*, 1984, Bodley Head) puts much greater emphasis upon the 'real' HF/DF as a technological winner (pp. 94–5) than he does upon 'Ultra' (pp. 134–7), which he tends merely to compare unfavourably with German code-breaking.

[2] Winton, John, 1988, *Ultra at Sea*, Leo Cooper, p. 118.

[3] Rohwer, J. & Hümmelchen, G., 1974, *Chronology of the War at Sea*, Vol. II, Military Book Society, p. 307.

[4] ADM 199/576.

[5] Levasseur, Jean, 1946, *Combats sur Mer*, Eds. J. Raymond et alii, France-Empire, pp. 82–7, 88–9; and ADM 199/575.

[6] *Ibid.*, p. 95.

[7] de Morsier, P., 1972, *Les Corvettes de la France Libre*, France-Empire, p. 252, note 1.

[8] Levasseur, *op. cit.*, pp. 97–8.

[9] *Ibid.*, p. 96.

[10] ADM 199/1145, written report by Lieutenant H. C. Briggs RNVR.

[11] *Ibid.*, written report by the Captain of ACONIT.

[12] *Ibid.*, written report by the Captain of ROSELYS.

[13] J. Rusbridger, 1991, *Who Sank Surcouf?*, Century, pp. 120–1.

[14] Rohwer & Hummelchen, *op. cit.*, p. 307.

[15] ADM 199/1145.

[16] Poolman, K., 1982, *Sea Hunters. Escort Carriers and U-boats 1941–45*, Arms & Armour Press, p. 28.

[17] Rohwer, J., 1977, *The Critical Convoy Battles of March 1943*, Ian Allan, p. 62.

[18] Admiral Sir Max Horton, ADM 199/575.

[19] Correlli Barnett, 1991, *Engage the Enemy More Closely*, Hodder & Stoughton, pp. 596–7.

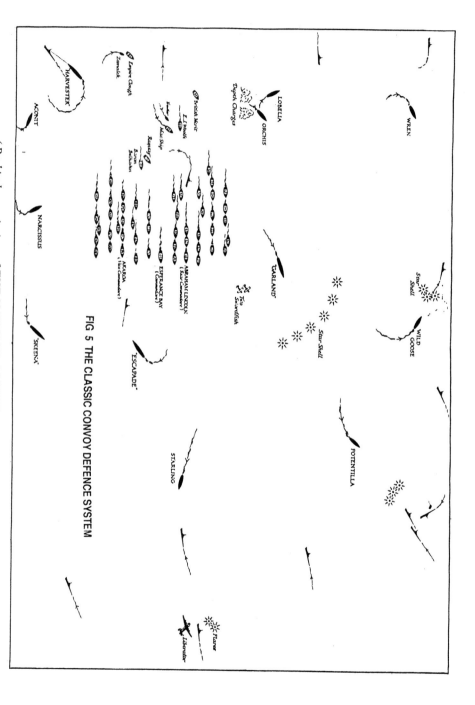

FIG 5 THE CLASSIC CONVOY DEFENCE SYSTEM

(By kind permission of THE NATIONAL MARITIME MUSEUM, LONDON)

CHAPTER 7

HX232 – The Trials of a Rescue Ship

The loss of HARVESTER and our Senior Officer brought a new leader, Commander M. J. Evans, RN; at first he and his small staff sailed in our other British destroyer, ESCAPADE, but HMS KEPPEL was soon procured to lead the Group. To give the new leader a feel of his group, exercises were arranged with a training submarine off the north coast of Ireland before the next convoy westwards, which was to be ON174. Apart from HARVESTER we were now without ACONIT, who was having her bow straightened after her heroic ramming and BURZA, too, was required elsewhere. The convoy would include two oilers and the rescue ship ACCRINGTON. To make up the numbers HMS AZALEA joined us temporarily. In view of what transpired on the return journey, she may not have been too grateful for the privilege; worse would befall her at Slapton Sands in 1944, but that is someone else's story.

The passage westwards was a quiet one, for the escorts anyway, enabling the new command structure to 'shake down'. Indeed, until September 1943 the longer outward journeys seemed to be more free from attacks. Whether this was because the enemy preferred to sink ships filled with war supplies rather than empty ones, or because the Germans got better information about the setting out of convoys from New York and Halifax, we never knew.

The weather during the crossing mirrored the drama which was being played out in the Commodore's ship: calm and 'fine for the first week and perfectly vile and foul for the remainder of the voyage; sometimes blizzards, gales, icebergs, fog and sometimes all combined.' The escorts detected the icebergs by Radar and then illuminated them by searchlight for the convoy to feel their way round. Surprisingly an average speed of 8.2 knots was maintained.

Not so surprising was the effect of all this upon the temper of the two leading seamen in the convoy, the Commodore and what, in the Royal Navy, would have been called his 'Flag-Captain'. Apparently the Master of the Commodore's ship, the MANCHESTER EXPORTER, questioned the authority of the Commodore over the switching on or off of the ship's navigation lights in fog. The Commodore was Vice-Admiral Sir Raymond Fitzmaurice, KBE, DSO, RN (Rtd.), and he carried his dissatisfaction all the way to the owners of the vessel. He concluded: 'I gathered from remarks passed by the Master that he had had a surfeit of Commodores. I am inclined to agree and suggest that he should be given a long holiday from them. This is the first occasion in 3½ years . . . 39 convoys . . . etc., etc.'

The unlucky official in the Trade Division of the Admiralty whose task it was to placate the Commodore, replied to him gently, asking him to let him write to owners of vessels in future, but agreeing with other suggestions, that ships with net defences should be relegated to slower convoys, that 4 cables apart was too far and that it should be reduced to 3 cables and so on. Sadly, before the completion of convoy ON174, the Commodore fell and broke his clavicle and had to be landed for hospital treatment on arrival in port.[1]

The wonder was not that the old men of the sea should get so testy, but that so many of them should be willing to give up their comfort and, in some cases, their lives. The proof of their effectiveness was in the perseverance of the convoys: as in other successful military enterprises, their subordinates were more afraid of them, in a jocular, bantering fashion, than they were of the enemy.

On 6 April the Group set out from St John's to meet convoy HX232. NARCISSUS was immediately in trouble, damaging her Asdic dome on ice, which was to be met in these latitudes, especially in the Spring thaw; she had to return to St John's. She was soon out again and, coming up astern of the convoy, thought she detected a shadowing U-boat on the Radar screen; after a fruitless night of chasing a will-o-the-wisp, it was believed that St Elmo's Fire at the masthead had been giving some false echoes! Radar was a powerful weapon, enabling a convoy's protectors to 'see' nighttime predators, but it could still play tricks.

HX232 comprised 48 ships in twelve columns; the Commodore was retired Rear-Admiral J. Powell, DSO, RN, in CITY OF ADELAIDE. There was no rescue ship allocated to the convoy and Commodore Powell was already fidgeting about the prescribed distance of 800 yards between ships in a column; he decided to revert to his preferred gap of 400 yards in order to discourage stragglers, amongst other reasons. His decision was subsequently justified by the achievement of an average overall convoy speed of 9.31 knots, despite experiencing a thick fog on 6 and 7 April.

A signal from the Admiralty to all the escort vessels of HX232 on 11 April advised that: 'D/F bearings . . . indicate probable patrol line of U/Bs from approximately 55°59'N 34°01'W to approximately 50°58'N 32°02'W'.[2] The convoy being on an east-north-easterly course and almost equidistant from Newfoundland, Great Britain and Iceland in mid-Atlantic, a glance at the ocean chart confirmed that there was no way round to be found. The only hope of avoidance of the reported patrol line lay in slipping in between the links along its huge length (over 350 miles); but, as Evans was subsequently to relate, '. . . a short enigma-bearing 179° and 337° respectively. . . thought to be the first sighting reports of HX232.'[3]

The patrol line, comprising ten U-boats of the LERCHE group, was in contact and, in the early morning of the 12th, U-563 and U-168 sank the freighters ULYSSES and PACIFIC

GROVE, which were carrying general stores and diesel oil. PACIFIC GROVE had been in a relatively dangerous position in the convoy, as the leading ship of the twelfth and outside column; but the crew of ULYSSES must have thought themselves well sheltered as the rear ship of the tenth column. According to a deck officer of NOAH WEBSTER, directly ahead of the unfortunate ULYSSES, the TUNGSHA (rear ship in the eleventh column) saw the U-boat coming down between the eleventh and twelfth columns and took action to avoid the torpedo, which went on to hit ULYSSES. This was not the only shenanigan of the night.

The second ship of the starboard wing (twelfth) column, FRESNO CITY (carrying tea, manganese ore and ground-nuts), was also hit right aft, leaving the 4-inch gun hanging over the side; the crew abandoned ship. HMS AZALEA was appointed rescue ship by the Senior Officer and set about the task. She saved all the crew, 40 men, of ULYSSES, 54 crew and 16 passengers from PACIFIC GROVE. When she got round to FRESNO CITY, she found the vessel still afloat and had to persuade the crew to row their boats back to the ship, so that they might at least destroy the confidential books which had been left on board. As they were about to do so, U-706, which must have only just arrived on the scene, put a further torpedo into the stopped ship and Lieutenant G. C. Geddes RNR, captain of AZALEA, finally picked up the merchant crew and called it a day.

His troubles, however, were not yet over. In his corvette, which would have carried between 80 and 100 men already in cramped conditions, he now hosted 158 extra survivors. People rescued by the Royal Navy are always fulsome in their praise for Jolly Jack's hospitality, however trying the circumstances and this occasion would have been no exception. It turned out that 8 of PACIFIC GROVE's 16 passengers were women; Lieutenant Geddes gallantly turned his slightly more spacious day-cabin over to them. The benevolence of this weary man was ultimately exhausted when he discovered that the husband of one of

HMS AZALEA, in April 1943 with convoy HX232.

the women was also among the survivors and that he did not, after such an ordeal, wish to be separated from his wife!

On AZALEA's return to the convoy, Commander Evans ordered her to make for the UK at full speed with her precious cargo. In his final report to Captain 'D', Geddes eschewed any comment on his problems with the passengers, but he rather pointedly selected only the Masters of ULYSSES and PACIFIC GROVE to be praised for 'coolness' and 'cheerfulness'.

The 12th April was not without further incident: Lieutenant de Fonbrune of RENONCULE, who had carried out an inconclusive attack on a U-boat the previous day, reported that the French corvette had been missed by two torpedoes across her port quarter. The convoy now came within range of liberator aircover from Aldergrove and between the planes and the escorts the U-boats were finally driven off.

ROSELYS too had encountered a U-boat in the early hours

of the 12th, had illuminated it with starshell and dropped depth-charges. This drew an eventual and constructive comment from Captain 'D' in Greenock to the effect that ships should consider using other means of illumination in order to leave the 4-inch gun to fire at the enemy. This undoubted gunlaying problem in a small warship, of elevating the barrel to fire starshell and then rapidly lowering it to lay back on to the target, was eventually solved by attaching illuminating-rocket rails to the 4-inch gun shield.

A successful convoy carrier action

On 22nd April 1943, NARCISSUS started her second annual refit in a slightly unusual location: passing through the spectacular islands off the west coast of Central Scotland, then east of the twin mounds of the Paps of Jura, through the Firth of Lorn and Loch Linnhe, past the town of Fort William backed by the monolith of Ben Nevis, on a brilliant and all too rare sunny Scottish Spring day, we came to Corpach. Sitting in the middle of Loch Eil was a floating dry-dock, into which the diminutive corvette was swallowed. Quite why the ship had to be hidden away in the heart of the Highlands for six weeks was never clear to us, because there seemed to be no major change envisaged in our armament or electronic detection gear, merely the usual retuning and repairing after a hard winter in the north Atlantic. The prospect of a laborious journey on the West Highland railway to Glasgow, for most to catch the express train south, did not dampen the crew's enthusiasm for the impending long leave which all would now enjoy in turn.

For the remainder of B3 Group it was business as usual. The outward-bound convoy avoided trouble, although threats at this time of year came not only from the enemy but from the thawing icefields of the north. Indeed, on the way inwards, the convoy Commodore of HX239, Sir A. J. Davies RNR, in the M/V RANGITATA, reported '2 large icebergs sighted 20 May in 48°N 43°20'W'; i.e. in a latitude south of the Scilly Isles, albeit in the West Atlantic!

The Group escorted convoy HX239 of 45 ships from 18 to 26 May and took part in what, in retrospect, can be seen as a very significant battle. The Senior Officer was now installed in HMS KEPPEL and he had the services of ESCAPADE as well as GARLAND, all four Free French corvettes as well as ORCHIS, HMT NORTHERN GEM escorting the rescue tug GROWLER but, best of all, he had the support of the 4th Support Group. This carrier group, comprising HMS ARCHER plus fleet destroyers and a sloop, was to see the convoy through that dangerous mid-Atlantic gap between the periods of daytime observation and reconnaissance that could be provided by land-based aircraft. Until such time as the carrier had to face upwind to fly off aircraft, she took station at the back of the seventh column.

The Commander U-boats, accurately informed of the convoy's whereabouts by his code-breaking service, directs the MOSEL group to intercept. Before it can do so, it is mauled by another escort carrier's aircraft, our erstwhile comrades in BOGUE. When the MOSEL group does approach HX239 it is found in mid-morning on the 23rd May by Swordfish and Martlet aircraft from ARCHER. U-752 is hit on the waterline by rockets: a first-use, first-time success for this weapon. U-752 cannot now submerge and when KEPPEL and ESCAPADE come up it is compelled to scuttle itself at 1050 hrs ESCAPADE picked up 13 survivors but had to leave 20 to 30 Germans who were, in her words, 'no longer buoyant'.

The only casualty on the British side was HM Trawler DANEMAN, which was found in a sinking condition by RENONCULE; after taking off the crew she had to be despatched by gunfire. The French Captain, de Fonbrune, deputed the task of burying two of the trawler's crew to his British Naval Liaison Officer. Commander Evans in HMS KEPPEL and the Commodore in SS RANGITATA were ecstatic in their praise for ARCHER's aircraft. On the day after the sinking of U-752, Dönitz, now in Paris having been removed there by Hitler's fear that the British raid on St Nazaire could be repeated at the U-boat HQ in Lorient, stopped the main Battle.

Meanwhile back at Loch Eil, in our dry-dock off Corpach, NARCISSUS was able to send both port and starboard watches on a fortnight's leave and advantage was taken by the Admiralty to acclimatize new officers. The fatherly First Lieutenant was replaced by the boisterous Trevor Jones. The other senior watchkeepers, Gray and Edye, also left, their places being taken by two brand-new Sub-Lieutenants, Roy Slater and Gordon Drew. It was some indication of the increasing productivity of the naval training establishments in the UK that, from now on, more and more officers and men could be provided for these little ships: hitherto the officer complement had been held at just six deck officers; after June 1943 NARCISSUS would carry up to ten officers, including engineers, or for training, experience, or just on passage.

On 5 June 1943, with the refit completed, NARCISSUS briefly became an Admiral's pinnace. Admiral H. R. Stark USN, the Commander United States Naval Forces in Europe wanted to look at how our Western Approaches base in Londonderry operated and we were designated to sprint him across the Irish Sea. He was not the only full admiral I had ever seen; we had, after all been inspected by the affable previous Commander-in-Chief, Western Approaches, Sir Percy Noble.

Yet I was sufficiently impressed, when I came down to the Wardroom during the crossing and found him sitting in an armchair asleep with his cap on, to consider taking a photograph of him in his full regalia. I very occasionally brought a borrowed camera to sea and was on the lookout for suitable subjects. But, in the same cursedly unadventurous spirit that had persuaded me not to continue that diary, which I had kept before my naval career began, I decided that it would be a republican form of *lèse majesté* to thus capture the poor man for posterity. I console myself now with the discovery that he was considered to be a lot more pro-British than the notorious Admiral Ernest J. King,

USN; Stark might have become less so if he had fallen victim to a uniformed *'paparazzo'*.

OS49 and KMS16; a tropical interlude

Whether it was a reward for the sinking of U-752 or, the more likely, whether the Admiralty had learned through Ultra that the southbound convoys faced the greater threat, we were pleased to have been kitted out during our sojourn at Corpach with tropical gear. NARCISSUS rejoined B3 Group directly from Londonderry and were glad to see the escort carrier HMS BATTLER and her consorts, TYRIAN and TUMULT, arrive on 6 June.

Our regular escort group of KEPPEL, BURZA and six corvettes was further reinforced on the 9th June by the cruiser GAMBIA, which stationed herself in a covering position 35 miles to eastward, i.e. between the convoy and probable enemy threats, whether from below or above the sea. An enemy seaplane did in fact intrude, but the Seafires flown off by BATTLER were distracted from their proper target by a friendly but unannounced Whitley, allowing the German to escape. No further intervention by the enemy occurred so, in the unusually calm waters of the Bay of Biscay, the four destroyers oiled from SS OLIGARCH on the 8th June and most of the corvettes were topped up on the 11th.

At 33°26'N, 9°49'W, i.e. off the African coast, 8 ships from Gibraltar and 5 from Casablanca joined; the escort was now down to two destroyers and four corvettes. Our journey south would have been entirely blissful if it had not been for a unique experience which, nevertheless, seems not to have been worth recording in the official reports. As the convoy was passing down the African coast in a flat calm sea it 'collided' with a swarm of locusts. The land was out of sight and a light wind blew off-shore.

In little time NARCISSUS was covered by four-inch long, crawling insects; so was the sea. What caused the locusts to come down at the moment we had no idea. Presumably they had been beating against an adverse wind for hours and thought that these strange lumps on the sea were islands. With all of us on the bridge rushing around tearing the insects off ourselves it was fortunate we did not run into anything; the helmsman was, of course, under cover and hurriedly closed the wheelhouse door which had been opened for air. Alas, British adaptability failed us on this occasion: a variation of our constant diet of corned beef and powdered potato would not now have come amiss. Had we but known it then, locusts are delicious when deep-fried and in batter! Even in the nineteenth century roasted locusts were credited with tasting like 'fried shrimps'.[4] Whether or not the Leading Cook of NARCISSUS could have been persuaded to allow them into his galley would have been another matter entirely.

The destroyers had to go, in turn, into Dakar and refuel on the 19th. In what seemed to us an exercise of sheer bravado, on the night of the 22nd motor launches pretended to be U-boats attacking the convoy. On the next day a local escort group took over 11 ships for onward passage to Takoradi and B3 Group escorted the remaining 16 ships into Freetown. The journey had proved longer than those we had been used to across the north Atlantic and for the whole of the 19-day passage the convoy was given air cover of one sort or another.

Freetown

The main attraction of Freetown for the British was the beach: a long stretch of rather gritty yellow-brown sand gave a rather more exotic flavour to the relaxation period between convoy escorts than we had become accustomed to. Others within the Group sought more substantial relief from the local palaces of pleasure. One comrade-in-arms claimed that all the others in his circle apart from himself had managed to acquire a certain ailment. 'It is of a more virulent form here than elsewhere,' he confided with apparent satisfaction. Aids had not then been discovered.

Freetown was not a posting sought by regular naval officers, I think, unless they had already given themselves up to that other source of consolation, alcohol. The slanderous rumour about the base-ship anchored alongside the main jetty was that she would be unable to put to sea ever again, being grounded on an underwater mountain of empty gin bottles.

SL132 and MKS16; the 'wireless silence' controversy starts

Anyone in B3 Group who wished to inflict serious damage upon themselves in Freetown was only given five days to do so, because by 28 June we were on our way back to the UK in a convoy of 57 ships under the supervision of Commodore Van den Donker in SS EURYBATES. Any notions, too, that the idyllic sunshine cruise which had brought us south would be repeated on the northward leg of the round trip were soon dispelled. Right outside the harbour boom a submerged U-boat was detected and attacked by KEPPEL and ACONIT. The latter stayed with the contact all night, only catching up the convoy after daylight. One break to the monotony of the southern convoys was their bus-line aspect: as the slow (6.5 knot) convoy passed various ports, a few ships shepherded by their local escorts would come out and a few would peel off and go in under protection. Dakar, Casablanca, Gibraltar, even Lisbon were often stages on the slow trek north or south.

On 6 July the crew of a Catalina reports that their aircraft has been damaged by a U-boat on the surface '15 miles ahead'. With a characteristic mixture of caution and dash, KEPPEL asks the convoy to make a 45° turn to port, hands over protection duties to NARCISSUS and proceeds ahead. When nothing can be found, she returns and the convoy steers to regain its track after dark. After her little adventure, KEPPEL finds herself short of oil; but the accompanying Royal Fleet Auxiliary, FORTOL, is inexperienced in oiling from astern and has stowed all her hoses, so KEPPEL steams off once again and arrives in Casablanca with 6 tons of oil remaining.

The Sierra Leone portion (SL 132) had acquired 5 ships from Dakar on 1 July and Gibraltar contributed a further 21 ships (MKS 16) on the 11th. Commander Evans in KEPPEL now disclosed, loudly and clearly to all who might be listening on the airwaves, how bare the convoy defences were. The Admiralty thereupon directed an unlucky incoming group, B1 comprising HMS HURRICANE and four corvettes, to support our now massive convoy: they had been looking forward to a quiet few days in Gibraltar! So they, and we too, had to oil in heavy weather from the now chastened FORTOL.

The Senior Officer B3 also got a flea in his ear from the Flag Officer Gibraltar: '[Convoy] SL 132 in not (R) not to break W/T silence.' This was probably the beginning of an uneasy relationship between FO Gibraltar and B3 Group which would fracture in the following year. Into the bargain the event signalled the start of a protracted whinge from Commander Evans about communications.

In his Report of Proceedings for this convoy, he complains about the difficulties in liaising with covering aircraft and suggests that: '1. all signals [advising about air-patrols] should contain Estimated Times of Arrival [of aircraft] and their call-signs; 2. aircraft should answer their call-signs; 3. all aircraft should flash their identity on approach; 4. all aircraft should listen out and test their Radio Telephones at least once per patrol.' The long tirade will eventually end with a plea against radio silence for the best Nelsonian reasons (e.g. 'Engage the enemy more closely').

When the convoy drew level with Cape Finisterre, which marks the north-western limit of the Iberian peninsula, a Canadian destroyer, HMCS IROQUOIS, gave further support for the crossing of the Bay of Biscay. On the same day, the 14th July, an aircraft reported sighting a raft ahead; from it HURRICANE picked up 6 German survivors from U-191, sunk by a previous aircraft two days before. On the 15th the situation was deemed safe enough for B1 Group to rush back to Gibraltar and for IROQUOIS to proceed to Plymouth.

All this time the convoy had been progressing slowly homewards, but not without problems of its own. Two separate ships in convoy had patients aboard suffering from malaria. Both were transferred to ships which carried doctors, but both unfortunately died. On 19 July ORCHIS drew the short straw and accompanied the Loch Ewe section to their destination. The remainder of B3 Group proceeded to the Clyde.

ONS15; back to the north Atlantic

As we wended our way westwards not too slowly with our next convoy (this 'slow' convoy managed to reach a speed of 8½ knots), the northern summer seemed peaceful enough for Commander Evans to indulge his favourite pastime of exercising his escort ships. Five of the merchant ships were carrying over 200 depth-charges between them; there were also three oilers and two rescue trawlers.

These ample safety margins of supply and security facilities were in themselves evidence that a turning point was being reached. Evans rightly ensured that these improvements were not just for show: the newly-converted oiler SS F. J. WOLFE gave KEPPEL 123 tons of fuel in one hour and ACONIT took 85 tons from the oiler in 50 minutes. The other corvettes practised transferring depth-charges at sea, one at a time, drawing the comment from the watching Evans that it looked 'highly dangerous in anything but fine weather.' An accompanying Merchant Aircraft Carrier, SS EMPIRE MACANDREW, flew off aircraft daily as a precautionary measure, although there was no U-boat activity.

NARCISSUS and ORCHIS in Gibraltar.

Signalmen using Aldis lamp (note FS ACONIT in the background).

On the 18th August TOWY led KEPPEL, NARCISSUS, ORCHIS and RENONCULE into the American base at Argentia in Newfoundland. One more bonus was still to come in that smiling summer: LOBELIA and ACONIT were permitted to 'complete with stores' (which probably meant 'stock up with barrels of wine') at the nearby French island of St Pierre, which ACONIT had helped to liberate in 1941. Then the latter was to proceed to New Orleans to refit; another little reward for her sterling work in March.

HS253; the end of an idyll

On 24 August B3 Group, which had moved up to St John's, left at night to rendezvous with a fast convoy (9.5 knots) in a thick fog on the Newfoundland Banks. The Commodore, Rear-Admiral CN Rayne RN (Rtd) in SS RUAHINE had his hands full with 55 ships and, when the fog dispersed, he had to cope with gales on the 28th and 31st. He had six stragglers and two ships in collision which had to be sent back to St John's; SS PLOMAR, the tailend ship in the third column lost a wireless operator overboard, who was lucky to be picked up by ORCHIS. It is little wonder that the Commodore put in an indignant report about too bright stern lights in ships, about the stragglers and about the discomforts of his own ship.

As for the Escort Group, our normal strength of frigate, four corvettes and a destroyer was bolstered by the Trawler FUSILIER and two rescue tugs, BUSTLER and HESPERIA. Everything had happened to that convoy, except U-boats; NARCISSUS and ORCHIS were glad to be sent away on 1 September to escort a group of 10 fast ships to their destinations. We might have imagined that all we would have to deal with from now on were the vagaries of the north Atlantic. If we did, our minds were soon disabused.

References

[1] ADM 199/583, ADM 199/2101.

[2] ADM 199/575, 199/576, 199/1706.

[3] ADM 199/575. In retrospect, it may seem strange that the name of the German cyphering machine should be mentioned openly, considering the 'ultra' precautions taken to prevent the Germans from finding out that we were reading their signals. It must be borne in mind that this reference appears in Evans's *written* report, but it does show that he knew about Enigma.

[4] Winston Churchill, 1973, *The River War*, NEL Books, p. 85.

Other unpublished sources for this chapter were: ADM 1/13739; 199/577, /578, /585, /1423, /1706; 237/4, /237, /800.

CHAPTER 8

ONS18/ON202: a Pyrrhic

'victory' which turned the tide[1]

The final realization by the Germans that there was no escape from defeat at sea and that there was an end of hope for a miraculous delivery from the gathering strength of the Allies, either came in mid-1943 or in early 1944. Even some British historians have been equivocal about the belief that the turning point in the Battle occurred in May 1943: for one thing, 'the biggest convoy disaster of the war'[2] (23 ships sunk from convoys HX229 and SC122) took place only two months before that date. Leaving that contrary evidence aside, the case for preferring a May turning point rests upon the undeniable facts that, during the April to July quarter of 1943, overall Allied shipping losses did fall, U-Boat sinkings did rise and Dönitz did recall the underseas fleet for re-equipment and re-training.

An opposing belief, that the more plausible turning point of the Battle comes in September, rests upon the immortal aphorism which says: 'It takes two to tango.' Illustrating this attitude was the situation in 1940 after Dunkirk: the judgement of the rest of the world was that Britain was beaten and might as well give in; similarly in mid-1942, the land battle in Africa appeared to be over in favour of the Germans. Subjectively however, the defeated British refused to accept their apparent fate either in 1940 or in 1942 and that judgement proved to be correct. Therefore it might be argued that the truly objective turning point of any context can only be by the mutual consent of the antagonists.

The re-launch of the offensive with new weapons

According to a German account, 'Though May 1943 is regarded by most commentators as marking the end of the U-Boat offensive, German leaders saw the situation at the time rather differently.'[3] Thus we may perceive the months soon after September 1943, as the date when the definitive erosion of U-Boat morale or effectiveness took place. In August 1943 it appeared to Dönitz that there was a distinct chance of wresting the initiative from the hitherto relentless pursuers of his submarines. Until May the tactics and techniques of the convoy defenders had been gaining for themselves a marked advantage over the wolf packs of U-Boats: new support groups had been able to hunt individual Boats to destruction; new long-distance aircraft armed with Radar and searchlights were harrying them from the time they left their Biscayan bases.

Now the predatory submarines were to turn upon their recent tormentors with new weapons, principally the so-called *Zaukönig*,[4] an acoustic torpedo. Once the warships had been dealt with, so went the theory, the riches they escorted would be plundered at leisure. If this secret 'king' of battles proved to have feet of clay, the resultant disappointment for the U-boats could become more of an incubus than the statistical setbacks of May. This acoustic torpedo homed automatically on to the noise of a ship's propeller, but only when that ship was going at a speed of between 7 and 17 knots. When the U-Boat groups were re-deployed into the North Atlantic early in September 1943, they also carried improved anti-aircraft armament, Radar beam detectors and decoys.

Convoys ONS18 and ON202 in September 1943

The first convoy escorts to face unknowingly the new threat comprised British, Canadian and Free French ships. B3 Group accompanying the slow outward-bound ONS18 convoy of 27 Merchant ships, included the destroyers HMS KEPPEL and ESCAPADE, one frigate TOWY, the corvettes NARCISSUS, ORCHIS, ROSELYS, LOBELIA and RENONCULE; the group also had the services of an armed trawler HMT NORTHERN FOAM and the merchant aircraft carrier EMPIRE MACALPINE.

The Canadian 2nd Escort Group (C2) accompanied the fast outward-bound ON202 convoy of 38 ships and included a Canadian destroyer and two corvettes, HMCS GATINEAU, DRUMHELLER and KAMLOOPS and a British destroyer and frigate and corvette, HMS ICARUS, LAGAN and POLYANTHUS.

British Admiralty signal codes had been broken by German decoders, *B-dienst*, who warned the Commander U-Boats of the large target presented by these two adjacent convoys. Dönitz directed the defiantly-named *LEUTHEN*[5] group of 20 U-Boats to lie in wait for them with their new weapons. The British Code and Cypher School at Bletchley Park had also deciphered the German naval signals and were able to warn the Commander-in-Chief, Western Approaches of the impending U-Boat attack. He ordered a change in the compass course to be followed by all ships in the convoy, long-range aircraft cover from Iceland and additional surface escort from the nearby Canadian 9th Support Group (9 SG). This comprised an old ex-American destroyer, HMCS ST CROIX, three corvettes, CHAMBLY, SACKVILLE and MORDEN, and a British frigate HMS ITCHEN, carrying the Senior Officer of 9 SG.

Thus a score of surface escorts faced a similar number of U-Boats. A Canadian Liberator aircraft from Iceland struck the first blow of the battle, sinking U-341. By 19 September 1943 the *LEUTHEN* group was living up to the U-boat Commander's expectations, making contact with the target of 65 merchant ships and setting about the task of stripping away its protective cover.

The first casualties

It has become obvious to all members of the crew of NARCISSUS that the tranquillity of the summer months of undisturbed escorting across the Atlantic is about to cease. At the midpoint, south of Greenland, the weather is calm and the visibility is poor, but both the wireless traffic from on shore and the radio-telephone traffic between ships has risen perceptibly.

Now other escort ships of convoy ONS18 are being sent out to attack U-Boats which have been located by ship-borne high-frequency direction finders (HF/DF), or by land-based aircraft. Their depth-charges, attempting to force the U-Boats to keep well below the surface while the convoy changes course, keeps the NARCISSUS's crew closed up at action stations almost continuously throughout the night. One anti-submarine attack goes disastrously wrong: the Hedgehog missiles on ESCAPADE detonate before leaving their mounting.[6] The ship has suffered many casualties, the least of which is the loss of her Captain's nose!

Later on, news comes that a converging fast convoy has lost one of its protectors, the frigate LAGAN, whose stern has mysteriously been blown off. For the other escort crews unusual developments like this one are disconcerting. Had the sailors at the sharp end of the Battle known that the 'boffins' at home would be able to provide instant protection from the bite of the *Zaunkönig*, morale in the warships might not have suffered such a jolt in the days to come. This antidote, however, could not be provided until the ships returned to their home bases.[7]

The next day, 20 September, while the two convoys slowly coalesce, NARCISSUS is sent off on HF/DF bearings to depth-charge detected U-Boats, so she falls well behind the convoys. At dusk she is recalled to form part of the night screen and returns at full speed, but zigzagging. Past midnight, on the way back, a report comes from the ship's Radar scanning-room that an echo on the screen has been at a constant thousand yards distance right astern for some time: a U-Boat is following our white stern-wash hoping, no doubt, to be led back to the convoy. Recalled to action stations and after the ship has been turned about to head straight back for the Radar contact, the 4-inch gun's crew fires starshell to illuminate the target. In the circle of light beneath a parachute flare a black tubular shape stands out: the conning-tower. It is now 0320 hours in the morning of 21 September and the captain of U-270, Paul von Otto, nonchalantly observes that the starshell is so well laid on to its target that it almost lands on the submarine's stern and continues burning underwater.[8] However, before a high explosive round can be fired, the conning-tower disappears and NARCISSUS's Asdic starts transmitting its underwater soundings:

'Echo . . . Red 45 degrees, 500 yards' — comes from the Asdic operator in the cabinet at the front of the bridge.

A U-boat now fires a torpedo at the charging corvette, whose Asdic operator sings out: 'Hydrophone effect — torpedo running!'

From the corvette's Captain: 'Port twenty — Start the attack — 'Midships — Steer 090'

NARCISSUS combs the track of the oncoming torpedo and drops a pattern of ten depth-charges over the U-Boat's estimated position. If, as German records show,[9] it was U-260 which missed NARCISSUS, then either U-260 and U-270 were working in tandem, or we came across U-260 by chance.

Contact is then lost and, in any case, the corvette is now needed to pick up survivors: the destroyer ST CROIX has been torpedoed by the U-Boat she was sent out to find; and the corvette POLYANTHUS, sent to pick up what is left of the Canadian crew is herself sunk.

The Fate of HMS ITCHEN

The British frigate ITCHEN is also preparing to rescue the crew of ST CROIX. At daylight the frigate Captain orders NARCISSUS to circle ITCHEN at high speed as the latter stops to pick up two boatloads of Canadians. He reasons, logically but very unfortunately as it transpires, that his larger ship's sick-bay facilities will cope more easily with the 80 survivors. The two ships then proceed to pick up the officer-of-the-watch of POLYANTHUS; Sub-Lieut. P. J. Young RNVR is the sole survivor out of perhaps 90 men and no doubt thinks himself fortunate to be so selected by Providence.

The two warships are now far behind the slowly progressing combined convoys. Racing back through the mist in line abreast and 500 yards apart, a Radar gremlin plays tricks on the careworn watchkeepers.

'Submarine echo 500 yards on the port beam of ITCHEN!' comes the alarm from the Radar cabin of NARCISSUS. ITCHEN is warned and she swings to port, but finds nothing. A little later the bridge signalman shouts that ITCHEN now reports a Radar contact 500 yards on our starboard beam.

'Hard-a-starboard — action stations!' but there is nothing. A double echo from each ship upon the other's Radar screen piles nervous reaction upon already over-stretched experience.

The next morning, spirits in the Allied escorts are lifted as the Senior Officer's ship, KEPPEL, locates U-229 out on the starboard side of the convoy and sinks her. The fog also lifts and, throughout the day, U-Boats fight it out with aircraft and with sorties of escorts from the convoy. Between 19 and 24 September 36 attacks will be made on U-boats by escorts, including 3 by NARCISSUS, once alone, once with KEPPEL and ITCHEN and once with ITCHEN. 9 attacks by aircraft will include 2 by Swordfish from EMPIRE MACALPINE, who further distinguish themselves by landing back in the thick fog. Even the trawler, NORTHERN

FOAM, has a busy time playing long-stop, trying to ram a U-boat which was sneaking into the convoy from behind and carrying out a promising depth-charge attack the next night.

With the fog gone and the night moonless, conditions will be ideal for the U-Boats to attack on the surface, where they can both see better and go faster. In the early evening NARCISSUS joins KEPPEL to put and keep down a U-Boat reported by HF/DF ahead of the convoy. But after nightfall the corvette is back in her station on the port bow of the convoy in the closer of the two rings of escorts. Behind her are the merchant ships and ahead of her is the extended screen, mostly comprising 9SG, with SACKVILLE on NARCISSUS's port bow and ITCHEN under a mile away on her starboard bow. Also ahead, of course, are the U-Boats.

A few minutes before midnight on 22 September the Captain of ITCHEN – a Senior Officer himself of 9SG, but now subordinate to the overall Senior Officer in KEPPEL – asks permission to illuminate a Radar contact ahead of the convoy with starshell. 'No,' replied KEPPEL, over the radio-telephone in a conversation clearly audible to everyone on the bridge of NARCISSUS,' we have given our position away already too often tonight. Close the contact and investigate.'

At four minutes to midnight a tragedy is enacted as if it were a theatrical drama: the darkened amphitheatre of the sea is lit up by a spotlight from the bridge of the ITCHEN highlighting the conning-tower of a U-Boat. Simultaneously, ITCHEN opens fire with all guns which will bear. Within a few seconds the spotlight disappears; as does ITCHEN, in an explosion which is visible all over the ocean.

As the convoy passes over the spot, one brave merchant-man, SS JAMES SMITH, stops to pick up Petty Officer Clark and Able Seaman Flood, both ex-HMS ITCHEN and Stoker Fisher, ex-HMCS ST CROIX from the water; they were to be the only men left from three ships' companies; Stoker Fisher thereby surviving his second torpedoing in three days.[10]

Four merchantmen were also lost that night, SSs

SKELBRED and OREGON EXPRESS in the 10th column, FORT JEMSEG in the 9th and STEEL VOYAGER leading the port wing column, making a total of six, with three escorts sunk and one irretrievably damaged; there were no losses thereafter and the cost to the Germans were three U-Boats sunk and others damaged. With such a final act as the sinking of ITCHEN provided, there would seem to be no reason to doubt a success for the Germans.

The Deceptions of Success

Three mysteries remained however: why was this not a significant victory for the re-launch of the U-Boat campaign; how did ITCHEN die; and when did the escort captains know what precautions to take?

Dönitz's response to the rising U-Boat losses in the Spring of 1943 had been one of tactical withdrawal. As in any other campaign, whether military or naval, he had recognized that reinforcing defeat was never the best option. The 'wolf packs' in the north Atlantic were withdrawn to re-arm, enabling them to rejoin the Battle in September with renewed confidence. This confidence was to be reflected in the exaggerated claims made by the attackers of convoy ONS18/ONS202. The U-Boats reported back to Dönitz that they had sunk twelve escort vessels definitely and three probably, by acoustic torpedo, plus nine merchantmen by more conventional weapons. The actual Allied losses were three escorts sunk and one put out of action and six merchant vessels sunk; the cost to Germany was three U-Boats sunk and three damaged.[11]

One basis for the submariners' optimism lay in the nature of the new weapon which they were using; the acoustic torpedo was designed to find its target with only the minimum guidance from the torpedoman. For tactical and self-preservatory reasons it was neither wise nor necessary for a U-Boat to remain on the surface after firing an acoustic torpedo. The subsequent explosion would seem to represent a hit upon an escort, whereas in reality several such torpedoes exploded on colliding with the turbulent wakes of some surface ships without damaging their hulls.

To this general flaw in the perception of the weapon as 'The Battle-Winner' could be added the particular spectacle of ITCHEN's demise: separate U-Boats on the surface that night witnessed the dramatic extinction of a hunting escort ship. One such U-Boat was U-260, whose Captain's diary exists to this day: '... 23 September [1943] at 0156 hours [Central German time, of course] ... a high stab of flame, a 300 metre high mushroom cloud stays put for a long time. It is the place where one of the two destroyers, seen twenty minutes before, has disappeared...'.[12] This was the collective visual proof of what they had been experiencing individually over the previous four days, often only through their listening devices.

As each surviving U-Boat captain transmitted his claim of kills to his Commander in Paris, a composite picture of success was built up which not only bolstered the morale of the wolf-packs but even persuaded Dönitz that ultimate victory was still within his grasp. So the same tactics were repeated with succeeding convoys, but with less and less success.

This was due partly to the loss of the surprise factor, but mainly to the technical and tactical counter-measures: to the towed 'Foxer' device, which simulated propeller noises thus diverting torpedoes from their intended targets; and to the 'creeping attack', devised by Captain F. J. Walker, which not only kept both escorts involved below the risky speeds of 7 to 17 knots, but also prevented U-boats from becoming aware that the threat to them was imminent.

The convoys and their escorts kept on coming. It was only in the following year that Dönitz finally recognized that the gambit of withdrawal from the Atlantic followed by the acoustic riposte had failed. So the true turning point of the Battle was not properly the high and suspended activity level in the Spring of 1943 but the false dawn of the following Autumn. The consequences of the September skirmish against convoy ONS18/ON202 were, in the first place, the perseverance with inadequate techniques by the U-Boat packs, which were to lead in turn to terminally dashed expectations and final disillusion.

Post-war Analysis of the Fate of HMS ITCHEN

How did ITCHEN meet her end? Most subsequent general histories of the Battle of the Atlantic give a brief account of the clash over Convoys ONS18/ON202, but many are confused about who did what in an admittedly confusing scenario. Whereas one account declares that 'U-666 fired two Gnats. One exploded astern of MORDEN, but the other *ran on* and hit ITCHEN, who blew up and sank.'[13]; another suggests that 'U-666 fires two T-5s, one of which exploded just to the stern of MORDEN, while the *second* hits and blows up the ITCHEN.'[14] (my emphases). These phrases, including the precedence given to MORDEN, ill accord with both U-666's account of what happened and with contemporary observation.

The Analysis of U-Boat Operations, based in part upon the convoy report by the Senior Officer in KEPPEL, is more specific:

'At 2335 MORDEN obtained a Radar contact which she chased across the front of the convoy. The contact faded but was picked up on the asdic and attacked with a 10-charge pattern at 2354. She turned to run in again but was forced to go to starboard to avoid collision with ITCHEN . . . ITCHEN . . . is known to have passed ahead of SACKVILLE and astern of NARCISSUS before being seen by MORDEN . . . . At 2359 ITCHEN, when ahead of No. 31 [leading ship in convoy column no. 3], switched on her 20-inch signalling projector and illuminated a U-Boat 300 to 400 yards ahead of her, steering about 030 degrees. At the same time she opened fire with her Oerlikon [20mm AA gun] and fired two rounds from her foremost [4-inch] gun. After about 15 seconds the signalling projector was extinguished and, perhaps a second later, there was a blinding flash as ITCHEN blew up.

When the U-Boat was illuminated, MORDEN had opened fire but owing to the close proximity of ITCHEN was unable to ram and lost it after the explosion'[15]

MORDEN was undoubtedly nearby, but the observer on NARCISSUS's bridge saw nothing of her participation and there is no mention in the Analysis of a torpedo exploding in her wake.

Professor Rohwer has no doubts about the destruction of ITCHEN: in his other painstaking work on German war-diaries he records that U-666 fired two acoustic torpedoes at four minutes to midnight on 22/23 September 1943. In an explanatory footnote to this statement, he writes:

'U-666 heard a Gnat detonation *after 8 minutes 21 seconds*; the torpedo detonated in the wake of HMCS MORDEN.

The *second* Gnat hit the ITCHEN after *1 minute 10 seconds; debris from this ship was later found on the conning tower of the U-boat.*'[16] (My emphasis)

From the information about debris and from the different lengths of torpedo running time, it is permissible to assume that U-666 had probably launched both her torpedoes before ITCHEN herself had opened fire; and that whereas one struck ITCHEN at point-blank range[17] the other, fired simultaneously, exploded harmlessly 6,000 yards further on. What seems to have caused confusion among historians were the phrases: 'The second Gnat hit the ITCHEN . . .', and 'the other ran on'; whereas this 'second' Gnat was the first to hit and did not have to 'run on'.

Could the escorts have been forewarned about Zaunkönig?

Quite apart from British research into and use of acoustic weapons, the Admiralty was both well-informed about the variety of torpedoes carried in U-boats and was aware of the threat of 'new weapons'; but, perhaps due to the reduced signal traffic between May and September 1943, or due to

Dönitz's success in camouflaging the emergence of a radically different torpedo, Ultra seems to have given the Admiralty little help in the opening phase of the acoustic battle.

In an intelligence report, dated 16 June 1943, an analysis of numbers and types of torpedo carried in U-boats, six specific types were listed: 112 U-boats carried 344 standard 21-inch air torpedoes, 497 21-inch electric ones, 73 FAT ('to-and-fro track'), 195 T3 and T2. T3 and T2 torpedoes were thought probably to be improved electric ones with longer ranges. There was no mention of T5 at this date.[18]

In his Weekly U-boat Situation report for the 20th September 1943, the Director of the Operational Intelligence Centre referred to that morning's torpedoing of LAGAN and ventured: 'It remains to be seen whether the talk of new weapons means anything . . . the nature of her [LAGAN's] damage may indicate the use of some type of acoustic torpedo, but there has been no indication in Special Intelligence [Ultra decrypts] that such a device has been perfected.'[19]

The same director also reported that U-boat commanders had been ordered to give 'misleading information' to their own crews about the new weapon, in the hope that this would prevent the British from gaining an insight, from future U-boat survivors, into its limitations. Even signals reporting attacks should be elaborately pre-coded.[20]

The Ultra decrypt which disclosed this curly ploy is only now available to us; its time of origin in U-boat headquarters was 1320 hours on 21 September 1943, but it was not decrypted until 2305 hours on 24 September, i.e. after the battle had been broken off. In this message Dönitz directed all U-boat commanders, when radioing the results of firing a *Zaunkönig* [T5], to report details in a 'disguised' fashion. They should '1. Add 50° to real track angle . . . 2. Give no details of enemy's speed which could reveal limits of performance of *Zaunkönig*. For "enemy speed too high" use keyword *"Koblenz"*, for "enemy speed too low" use keyword *"Trier"*. 3. Firing data and limits must be kept secret from the crew. If necessary produce the impression that the best defence against *Zaunkönig* is afforded by enemy speed of less than 15 knots.'[21] Thus did the wily Dönitz outmanoeuvre himself, setting a disinformation trap; the decrypt of this finesse was too late to save ST CROIX, POLYANTHUS and ITCHEN, but it ensured that, in succeeding battles, the odds were loaded in favour of the escorts.

An unfortunately-timed message from the Admiralty

A remaining mystery concerns the timing of the warnings from the Admiralty that acoustic torpedoes might be used and how the risk they imposed might be minimized.

Clearly no signal was sent to Senior Officers of the three Groups involved until the ST CROIX and POLYANTHUS had been sunk on 20 September. When the captain of NARCISSUS subsequently gave evidence to the Canadian Board of Inquiry into the losses, he started: '[at 2346 on the 20th] ITCHEN told us that on no account were we to go slow as he imagined that was how POLYANTHUS had been torpedoed, *which I understand is not the case now.*' (my emphasis).

On the other hand, we know that an Admiralty signal was sent by 0215 the next morning because Commander Evans, in his written report to the C-in-C Western Approaches, said 'ICARUS obtained Radar contact at 5000 yards and chased the submarine. Unfortunately at that moment he (ICARUS) was shown the latest Admiralty advice on combating the new German weapon and this dissuaded him from closing the range until the submarine dived some 12 miles away from the convoy.'[22]

The Admiralty message was referred to again by the captain of one of the ships of B3 Group as the reason for closing and boarding the Senior Officer's ship, in the middle of the battle, for a face-to-face conference: '... bearing in mind the possible danger of acoustic torpedo as notified by Admiralty's three messages of September 20...'[23] This unusual confrontation was to cost that particular escort captain his command for, on arrival in Newfoundland he was relieved 'without explanation.'

It was Captain (D), St John's himself who arrived on board to impart the bad news to the Captain of ROSELYS. The French crew evidently knew what was afoot and thought their Captain was being hard done by. Captain (D) somewhat marred the solemnity of the occasion by asking, at the gangway, to be taken 'to the madman'. The officer of the watch responded grimly with 'Which madman? We have 90 on board.'[24]

As for the Admiralty's timing, it must on this occasion qualify for the aphorism 'the road to hell is paved with good intentions': its tardiness failed to warn one captain of the danger he was facing; its arrival put another captain off his stroke; and it so rattled a third that he lost the confidence of his Senior Officer and, consequently, command of his vessel. This message, advising how to deal with the acoustic torpedo, does not quite deserve to be placed in such a disastrous category as the notorious 'Scatter!' signal to convoy PQ17, but should it be debited against the 'Ultra' secret? Not in the long run, I believe.

The W/T silence, which was imposed upon the U-boats until the combined convoy ONS18/ON202 was met, gave the Germans an initial advantage, but Dönitz gave the game away with his directive about 'enemy speeds'. Once he had committed *Zaunkönig*'s weaknesses to the airwaves, Ultra opened his hand of cards for his opponents to trump quite often.

References

[1] An earlier version of this chapter appeared in the *Mariner's Mirror*, 1993, Vol. 79, pp. 325–31.
[2] F. H. Hinsley et al., 1981, *British Intelligence in the Second World War*, Vol. 2, HMSO, pp. 548–9; 562.
[3] Jak Mallman Showell, 1989, *U-Boat Command and the Battle of the Atlantic*, Conway Maritime Press, p. 158.

[4] Literally 'Hedge-king'; somewhat ironically meaning 'Wren' in German, but designated T-5 or GNAT by the British. Commander Peter Cremer, a U-boat captain who survived the War, tells us that U-boats were only armed with 4 T-5s initially: see his *U333. The Story of a U-boat Ace*. 1984, Bodley Head, p. 150.

[5] Named after a military victory by Frederick the Great over the Austrians. It may be significant that this land victory was known by the Germans to have been gained against all the odds (see Showell p. 167).

[6] According to the planned characteristics of the weapon, the fuse of each missile should not have been armed until it had travelled 10 feet through the water; see ADM 199/2058. The 'buzz' at the time was that 'someone', unspecified, could have caused the accident by idly spinning the tiny impeller on the uncapped nose of one missile!

[7] Hinsley, *op. cit.*, Vol. 3, part 4, p. 223.

[8] *War Diary*, U-270, held on reel 1095, Foreign Documents Section, Ministry of Defence, London.

[9] J. Rohwer & G. Hümmelchen, 1974, *Chronology of the War at Sea*, Vol. II, Military Book Society, p. 354.

[10] Marc Milner, 1985, *North Atlantic Run, The Royal Canadian Navy and the Battle for the Convoys*, Toronto, p. 274.

[11] Ministry of Defence, 1989, *The U-Boat War in the Atlantic, September 1943 – February 1944*, Chapter VIII, p. 26–27.

[12] *War Diary*, U-260, held on reel 1094, Foreign Documents Section, Ministry of Defence.

[13] John Winton, 1988, *Ultra at Sea*, Leo Cooper, p. 158.

[14] Rohwer & Hümmelchen, *op. cit.*, Vol. II, p. 355.

[15] ADM 199/2060.

[16] J. Rohwer, 1983, *Axis Submarine Successes*, Patrick Stephens, p. 172 and Note 17.

[17] 'The German acoustic torpedo had an arming range of 400 metres, this being the distance a torpedo had to travel before the detonators could activate the explosive.' Showell, *op. cit.*, p. 169.

[18] ADM 223/4.

[19] ADM 223/18, p. 72.

[20] *Ibid.*, pp. 68/9.

[21] *DEFE* 3/722.

[22] ADM 199/353.

[23] *Ibid.*

[24] Personal communication from M. Maurice Jacon, ex-ROSELYS.

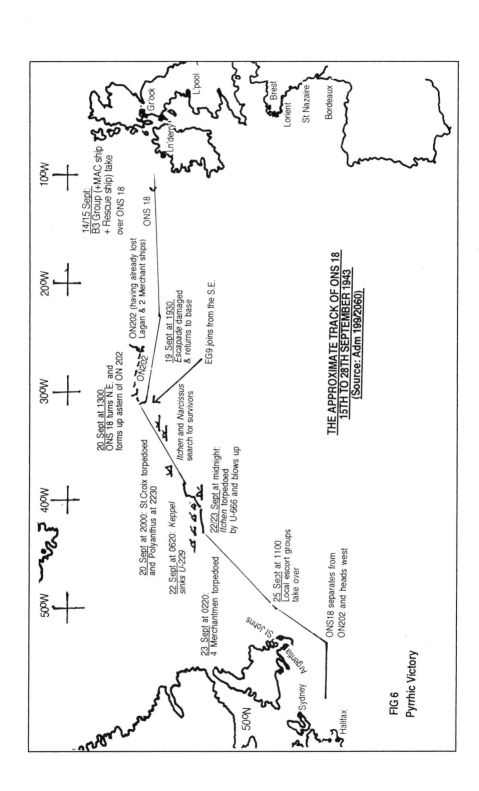

THE APPROXIMATE TRACK OF ONS 18
15TH TO 28TH SEPTEMBER 1943
(Source: Adm 199/2060)

14/15 Sept:
B3 Group (+MAC ship)
+ Rescue ship) take
over ONS 18

ONS 18

ON202 (having already lost
Lagan & 2 Merchant ships)

20 Sept at 1300:
ONS 18 turns N.E. and
forms up astern of ON 202

19 Sept at 1930:
Escapade damaged
& returns to base

EG9 joins from the S.E.

Itchen and Narcissus
search for survivors

20 Sept at 2000: St.Croix torpedoed
and Polyanthus at 2230

22/23 Sept at midnight:
Itchen torpedoed
by U-666 and blows up

22 Sept at 0620: Keppel
sinks U-229

23 Sept at 0220:
4 Merchantmen torpedoed

25 Sept at 1100
Local escort groups
take over

ONS18 separates from
ON202 and heads west

St Johns

Argentia

Sydney

Halifax

Gr'ock

Ln'derry

L'pool

Brest

Lorient

St Nazaire

Bordeaux

100W

200W

300W

400W

500W

500N

FIG 6
Pyrrhic Victory

CHAPTER 9

Farewell to the North Atlantic

For the senior officers and captains of B3 Group the stop-over in St John's, Newfoundland, after the traumatic events of September 1943, was filled with courts of Inquiry into the loss of the three escort ships and also, doubtless, with anxious consultations as to any counter-measures to be taken against the new acoustic threat. If it had not been for the extreme sensitivity of the Ultra secret, I am sure we would all have been told that the antidote to the *Zaunkönig* torpedo was even now being supplied to ships in the UK.

In the absence of such reassurance, the crew had recourse to the hospitable bars of St John's and the officers to the wooden eyrie of The Buzzard's Crutch. Then, on 4 October, the Group filed out of the sheer-sided, narrow gap in the granite cliffs which forms the entrance to St John's harbour. The Senior Officer had now transferred himself to the River-class frigate, HMS TOWY, but still retained the destroyer KEPPEL as well as his five faithful corvettes, together with HM Trawler, NORTHERN FOAM. Trawlers were a great stop-gap early in the War, when escorts were few and far between, but they were slow and tended to rouse the ire of Senior Officers for making too much smoke! As more and more frigates came into services, armed trawlers could be spared from ocean escort work.

HX259

Although nominally routed from Halifax, elements of this convoy had left New York on the 28th of September and had already had an adventure: two RAF ratings, taking passage in one of the merchant ships, fell overboard while skylarking and were fortunate to be picked up by one of the local escort ships. This clearly did nothing to soften the temper of Commodore CA Fremantle, DSO, RNR in SS RIMUTAKA, whose fast convoy of 48 ships was to suffer, in the days to come, no fewer than 14 stragglers of whom only half returned to the fold. One of the returnees, the HENRY BACON (allocated to no. 33 position, i.e. third ship in the third column), luckily was able to rejoin after the absence of three days astern of the convoy.

Stragglers and 'rompers' (those ships which felt uneasy at the convoy speed and romped ahead at the first sign of trouble) frequently proved to be easy meat for the wolf packs. Rompers tended to start in the front rank of the convoy anyway; they were the faster, newer ships, and were probably tempted to press ahead. Whereas the stragglers were those who had been consigned to the rear rank and failed to keep up; although some stragglers seemed to be more dozy than delinquent.

Such was probably the case of the SS J. R. PARK, fourth ship in the seventh column of HX259, whose Master, when upbraided by the Commodore for straggling, responded then when he, the Master of J. R. PARK, had left the bridge at 1 o'clock in the morning of the 4th October his ship 'was then with the Convoy'. Commodore Fremantle thereupon crustily informed the Master of J. R. PARK, in a classic example of displaced aggression, that 'the officer in whose charge his ship was left was not to be congratulated.'[1]

B3 Group, as the Ocean Escort, had taken over the convoy from the local escort at 1530 hours on 4 October in the customary area east of Newfoundland. The only incidents in the next 24 hours were the ordered return to St John's of the SS STANLEY MATTHEWS with boiler trouble and the taking on of 80 tons of fuel by KEPPEL.

The remainder of the crossing was short and relatively sweet, untroubled by the enemy. What we did not know at the time, of course, was that another eastbound convoy, SC143, was allowed to engage a known group of U-boats '. . . in order to ensure a safe passage for HX259, a larger and more weakly escorted convoy, and the result [, the loss of one merchantman and one escort in sinking 3 U-boats, was] highly satisfactory.'[2]

Perhaps part of our 'weakness' was the mauling we had received with ONS18 the previous month and we had yet to have fitted the morale-boosting 'Foxers'. At the end of this homeward-bound convoy we would receive a supply of hollow metal tubes to be used in pairs and in parallel; when they were trailed well astern of a warship at sea, they would emit a booming rattle similar enough to the noise made underwater by a ship's propellor to attract an acoustic torpedo away from the ship's hull. Peter Cremer, a U-boat captain, has claimed to be the first German to hear the device, which his translator describes variously as a 'buzz', a 'howl' and a 'hum'.[3] His date of April 1944, however, seems much too late: I am positive that the 'Foxers' were waiting for us to use as soon as we had arrived back on the Clyde in October 1943.

The escorts of SC143 had clearly profited from the Ultra decrypts about the importance of low speed for targets of the *Zaunkönig*. More important, however, than the cumbersome 'Foxers' were the defensive, and ultimately offensive, tactics which were to flow from knowledge of that speed factor: they culminated in the famous and, for the U-boats, fatal tactic of the 'creeping attack'; but that is a later story.

The policy of non-avoidance of U-boat attack for strategic purposes is also interesting, because it foreshadowed what was to become the high-risk strategy of regularly inviting attack in the Bay of Biscay later.

Just before coming up to the point in the Western Approaches to the United Kingdom where HX259 could safely disperse, a minor sort of 'trouble' loomed for us; the

Senior Officer conducted a brief exercise of the Group's communication skills. We should have taken more notice then of the new commander's style so that, a few months later, we could have been better forearmed to cope with him.

ON208

25 October 1943 saw us with another 'Outward North-bound' fast convoy of 43 ships, achieving the giddy overall advance of 9.4 knots. The Commodore, in REINHOLT, was the redoubtable E. K. Boddam-Whetham, CBE, DSO, a man never fated to be overcome by the enemy, but who was to succumb to a tropical malady at a later date. For once all six of the regular corvettes were on parade and TOWY also had the services of the sloops KITE and WHIMBREL as well as no fewer than three rescue ships. Unseasonably, our crossing saw no fireworks, no smoke, no fog and no attacks by the enemy. Ahead of us, B7, a fellow Ocean Escort Group acting as support group, sank a U-boat. No losses of freighters occurred, but several dropped out due to 'shifting ballast' in the gallop westwards.

SC146

The returning November convoy (Commodore A. Cocks, RNR, in RENA) was surprisingly slower, taking all of 13 days: homecoming convoys often bounded along in front of an eastward swell and wind. Nevertheless it suffered no attacks, although one emergency turn to starboard was ordered just before dawn on the 17th; thanks, possibly, to Ultra decrypts which, we are now told, had been working smoothly, and in time to be acted upon, since the summer.

We seemed to have lost the services of RENONCULE on this leg. We thought that it was probably her turn to enjoy the Gallic charms of St Pierre. In fact she had done much better than most of her sister-ships: she was on her way down to a refit in New Orleans. We were more than compensated, however, by the presence of the 7th Support Group, comprising the escort carrier BITER and her consorting sloops, PHEASANT, CRANE, and CHANTICLEER. BITER lost a Swordfish aircraft, the only casualty.

Despite the depredations of September 1943, an indication of the growing strength of the Navy's control of the escort battle now made itself felt. There had been a foretaste of this phenomenon the previous May when two of the senior watchkeepers left the ship, at the end of their two-year stints, to take up new appointments. Peter Gray had gone to a new 'River' class frigate, USK, and Reg Edye had gone to a 'Loch' class, LOCH ALVIE.

Now, in December 1943, our first Captain was replaced by an ex-trawler captain and went to take over a new frigate of the American-built 'Captain' class. During the succeeding months two Engineer officers arrived; the first was a cheerful South African, Leonard O'Reilly, who would eventually be needed to take over the powering of a new 'Castle' class corvette. All these upward postings of experienced officers betokened the rapid increase in the number of ships becoming available to hunt U-boats and eventually to overwhelm them.

Shortly before he left, this seemingly withdrawn man, my first Captain, handed me a flimsy piece of paper which declared that I was fit to maintain a watch on a ship of the Royal Navy; he must, moreover, have sent a copy through channels to the Admiralty. Since I had been standing a watch for at least the last six months on my own. I probably did not give it much thought at the time. Unbeknown to me, however, I had initially been placed in that bible of precedence, The Navy List, in an alarmingly lowly group: Temporary Acting Sub/Lieutenants who were additionally 'Probationary'.

What this last epithet meant I never did discover, but I suspect that it was the Admiralty's way of covering itself in case I turned out to be a complete lemon and an aberration on the part of my sponsor, the Naval Attaché in Rio de

Janeiro. In which case no doubt I could have been jettisoned unceremoniously without the expense of returning me to Brazil. I was eventually gratified to find the Italic initials 'W/K' against my name in Navy Lists, which subsequently followed me on to the giddy heights of the Temporary Acting Lieutenant RNVR list for 1944, after I had served my two years as a Sub/Lieutenant. So I now feel guiltily grateful to a man whose qualities I had obviously not appreciated at the time!

OS61/KMS35

We did not know it then, but B3 Group had taken its last passage westwards: either the traffic returning from the Mediterranean for D-Day had assumed a greater importance than the flow of goods crossing the Atlantic, or the higher strategists had decided to take on the U-boats closer to their bases. At all events, the Group was now to play full-time on the Biscayan stage, for which the trip to Freetown the previous summer had been an unconscious rehearsal. The 'forward defence' thesis gains some credence from the greatly enhanced support now available; it was not yet a case of the escorts outnumbering the freighters but there was now an embarrassment of riches, compared with our previous poverty in the North Atlantic.

'Outward Southbound' convoy number 61/'UK to Mediterranean' convoy number 35, lasting from 2 to 21 December, comprised 46 ships in 14 columns of 5, with the Commodore, J. K. Brooke, RNR, in SOBO, heading the by now customary hollow column into which the carrier support could slot. This role was to be filled by HMS FENCER for the dangerous period between 12 and 17 of December. There were three rescue ships: LADY MADELEINE, SAPPER and PINTO. There was a rescue tug, ASSIDUOUS and the anti-aircraft ship PRINCE ROBERT. To round it off came TOWY, BURZA and 5 of the 6 corvettes – RENON-CULE had not caught us up yet. If this was a challenge, it is not surprising that neither the U-boats nor the Luftwaffe took it up.

The only hazard the convoy encountered was fog in the Irish sea, which held it up for a couple of days. The tranquillity of the passage thereafter was marred only by crises unrelated to the enemy. One rather touching signal was passed through the Senior Officer of the escort to the Dutch Captain of the Motor Vessel MADOERA: to the effect that the wife of Third Engineer Dehaans was critically ill in New York and that her health would benefit from a comforting message from him. This was duly passed back through the Senior Officer and the C-in-C Western Approaches.

In view of the communication difficulties and the hard times in which it occurred, this humanitarian concern is slightly astonishing; the feeling of surprise becomes less appropriate when one discovers, among the Enigma signals decrypted and translated at Bletchley Park at some expense and trouble, several telegrams of congratulations on the birth of children to members of U-boat crews at sea. Both the Allies and the Germans evidently recognized the power of warm gestures in the maintenance of morale. I wonder if British reserve ever permitted such breaches of customary phlegm and privacy? I cannot say that I can recall our poor Chief Bos'n's Mate receiving any congratulatory signal; he was allowed to get on with his solitary *couvade* undisturbed!

On 11 December TOWY's medical officer was transferred to a merchantman whose chief steward had fallen heavily and had seriously injured himself internally. Four days later the poor man died and was buried at sea.

On 21 December 1943 the convoy reached Gibraltar; the previous day had been my twenty-first birthday. In the context of almost daily tragedies, no-one spoke of birthdays and my own was no exception.

On this, our first arrival in Gibraltar, we became aware quickly of something unusual: the harbour entrance was relatively narrow and every few minutes, day and night, an underwater explosion could be heard inside the harbour. On enquiry, the whole story of Italian attacks upon Allied shipping in the vicinity of Gibraltar was revealed. During 1942 frogmen and 'human torpedoes' had crossed the Bay, often making use of an Italian ship, the OLTERRA, in Algeciras which had been specially modified to conceal the Italian sabotage teams. Although those early attacks had been directed at merchant ships anchored outside the harbour, precautions still had to be taken to deter a similar penetration of the harbour itself; hence the regular dropping of five-pound charges in the entrance at the end of 1943.

References

[1] ADM 199/577, 199/578.
[2] ADM 223/18, p. 60.
[3] Cremer, *op. cit.*, p. 175.

Other unpublished sources used in this chapter are: ADM/ 187/30; ADM 199/584 & 1336, 1812, 2101; ADM 237/159.

CHAPTER 10

The Gibraltar Convoys. Trailing our coat across Biscay

The years 1940 and 1941 had been years of unremitting disaster for Britain, for the Royal Navy, as well as for that umbilical cord of the nation and that microcosm of the Navy, the ocean convoy escort system. One has only to consider the catastrophes of Dunkirk, Greece, Crete and Singapore; to ponder the sinkings of the ROYAL OAK, COURA-GEOUS, BARHAM, REPULSE and PRINCE OF WALES; to weigh the loss of 4 million five hundred and sixty-six thousand tons of merchant shipping lost to U-boat attack.[1]

The years 1942 and 1943 can also now be seen as years of dour defence and continuing sacrifice: in the introspective world of the North Atlantic we have already seen the experience of B3 Ocean Escort Group and the price of Admiralty represented by the loss of HARVESTER and by the loss of ITCHEN and others. In contrast and at last, 1944 was to be the year not only of irreversible success but of a change of mood and of tactic. The time for escape and evasion and limitation of damage was over; there came about a subtle conversion of defiance into challenge, of avoidance of the enemy into his deliberate entrapment. This, of course, was only now possible because of the massive increase of resources coming from the powerhouse of the United States; risks could be taken with materials because of their relatively easy replacement. Innate caution with men's lives still remained; but a life risked now might save two lives later.

MKS34/SL143

These things are easy to see in retrospect, yet as B3 Group set out from Gibraltar at 0900 hours on Christmas Eve 1943 to take convoy MKS34 to its junction with the northbound SL143, not much seemed to have changed from the previous trip. The Group had its customary Senior Officer in TOWY, the Polish BURZA was present as were four of the regular corvettes; temporarily attached were the frigate WIND-RUSH and the trawler LADY MADELEINE. This escort conducted the Gibraltar portion to its meeting with the Sierra Leone section off Cape St Vincent, the most south-westerly point of land in all Europe.

This whole procedure was quite familiar to us by this time; it became increasingly clear by the 29th December, however, that it was not just the oranges in some of the ships which made this convoy special. On that day the escort carrier HMS STRIKER joined, with her escort screen, TWEED and WATCHMAN. The carrier was to operate her aircraft clear of the convoy by day but remain inside the convoy by night, in the usual way. Then on the 30th we were further gratified to find that a support group, the 6th E. G. comprising two British frigates and four Canadian corvettes, had joined us as an extended screen. By this time we were up level with the Bay of Biscay and found that Wellington aircraft were active to the east of us, making things as difficult as possible for the U-boats trying to slip out of Lorient, St Nazaire, La Pallice and Bordeaux before traversing the Bay. These additional defences could now only come to the attention of the individual ships of the close escort by observation, for the Admiralty had recently forbidden temporarily the use of the Radio/Telephone between the ships of the escort by imposing 'State Yoke' by radio.

On the same day as our Canadian friends arrived, one of

the ships in convoy, SS STANHOPE reported to the Commodore that a time-bomb had exploded in the hold; the ship had loaded oranges in Seville! More time-bombs went off the next day in both STANHOPE and SS EMPIRE HEYWOOD, which had taken on oranges and onions in Valencia. On 2nd January further explosions blew off the hatchcover of no. 1 hold in STANHOPE, but neither ship's hull was damaged in any way.[2]

On New Year's Eve and then on New Year's Day 1944, we noticed that the Group leader, TOWY, transferred fuel-oil first to HMCS SNOWBERRY, one of the 'guest' corvettes and then to HMCS LUNENBURG, another Canadian. Since low fuel consumption was supposed to be one of the virtues of a corvette, this surprised us. It was only much later that it became known that their group had joined us directly after a complex operation which had now used up their reserves.

This operation discloses the changed mood which had taken place almost imperceptibly in the Battle of the Atlantic. One of the few surviving German blockade-runners, the ALSTERUFER, had been 'sighted' making for the Gironde in SW France and a flotilla of German destroyers had been deployed to escort her in. Both ship movements are said to have been discovered by air recon-naissance,[3] but German naval signals were now being regularly decoded by Bletchley Park; if HF/DF detection of U-boat signals was being used to cover 'Ultra' secret decrypts of the Enigma code as Hinsley suggests (see chapter 6 above), then so might 'air reconnaissance' have been a cover story. The outcome of the discovery of the German ship movements was that the ALSTERUFER was sunk by a Czech-manned bomber of 311 Squadron, RAF, before she could either reach port or come under the pro-tective anti-aircraft fire of the destroyers; whilst the latter found themselves intercepted by the British cruisers GLASGOW and ENTERPRISE, who sank three of them. The Canadia corvettes had been spending their time and using up their fuel prior to joining us in searching for survivors from the four ships. They did in fact pick up 62 German sailors.

On 3 January, the convoy having passed through or round the 'BORKUM' patrol line of 9 U-boats without mishap, 6th E. G. was recalled to their base in Londonderry. When Commander Evans got back to base he voiced what seemed then to be a novel complaint about the imposition of R/T silence, on orders from the Admiralty at the beginning of the crossing of the Bay.

Senior Officers, necessarily one supposes, customarily kept their confidential knowledge to a very small circle of subordinates: our late leader, Commander Tait, may or may not have known that the advice he was getting from the Admiralty about U-boat dispositions was directly from decrypts of German signals. In the case of Commander Evans, perhaps what may have appeared to us as brash triumphalism, in renouncing the protection of silence on the airwaves, was merely his way of getting his colleagues used to a change in attitude. From his perspective, our current material advantages must now be pressed home with aggressive force; the time for defensive thinking was over.

OS65/KMS39

The succeeding southward-bound convoy over what had now become B3 Group's regular route was undistinguished from a martial point of view but became, for a number of NARCISSUS's ship's company, an era of even greater discomfort. The shortages in manpower and equipment in the previous three years of the Battle had begun to give way: the loading into these little ships of more powerful and effective weapons of defence and offence was accompanied, naturally, with an increase in the numbers of crewmen.

The corvettes themselves had been lengthened, at one of the yearly refits, in order to help them cope with those deep Atlantic rollers which they had not at first been intended to traverse. The longer forecastle also enabled more ratings to swing their hammocks on the Lower Deck.

The officers' cabins, too, were enlarged so that watch-keepers could double up, could give passage to the many officers travelling to or from harbours, or accommodate the new wave of technical experts or merely tyro 'salt-horses' borne for training. The sparse days in the North Atlantic of a wardroom 'front five' comprising Captain, First Lieutenant and three watchkeepers became, in later years, an over-full 'scrum' of six deck officers, two engineer officers plus, occasionally, a couple of passengers.

On one occasion NARCISSUS carried a brand-new Sub-Lieutenant, who gave every indication of never having been to sea before: he was very sick and seemed to have become very frightened. Perhaps we should call him 'X'. A watchkeeper, appearing unexpectedly at the wardroom door, might catch 'X' backing hastily away from the wardroom drinks cabinet. Although the consolations of alcohol were resorted to in harbour, it was an unwritten rule that no officer drank at sea, for obvious reasons; the ratings enjoyed a carefully regulated and watered tot of rum daily (and tried every trick in the book to circumvent both its compulsory dilution and immediate consumption), but the officers were quite aware of the potentially frightful conse-quences of drinking and 'driving'.

On arrival in Gibraltar, 'X' went ashore as soon as he was given leave to do so and reappeared eventually considerably worse for wear. The next morning the officer whose duties included that of Mess Fund Treasurer summoned a meeting of wardroom members and, in sepulchral tones, announced not only a discrepancy in the bar stocks but also the disap-pearance altogether of the petty-cash box. He mysteriously admitted that he had a good idea what had happened to both but would not, when pressed to explain himself, say anything further; which was an unsatisfactory state of affairs as every member now felt himself to be under suspicion.

The Mess Treasurer was saved further urging from his colleagues by a member of the crew, who came quite independently to the First Lieutenant and told him that, on the ship's arrival alongside the dock in harbour, he had observed 'X' to come up on deck and to throw what he thought to be a cash-box into the water. There was a certain link between the informant and 'X', so perhaps the former thought the latter was 'letting the side down'.

The First Lieutenant had no trouble in acquiring a diver from the dockyard, who soon retrieved the tin box. When faced with this evidence, the desperate 'X' confessed all. Where trouble really began was when the Captain tried to get 'X' accepted ashore for Court Martial. The Senior Officer ashore dumfounded everyone by saying that he had no facilities for court-martialling an officer and, amazingly, that NARCISSUS was to take him onwards for disposal! This suited nobody, least of all the unhappy 'X' who, quite apart from the indignity, was going to have to suffer in reverse what he had been trying to blot out over the previous period, i.e. the hazardous passage of the ocean. The subsequent trip was a nightmare for all concerned: 'X' had to be confined to his cabin except for meals which he had to take with his erstwhile colleagues, for the two stewards had quite enough to do without being loaded with the extra work of separate sittings. Facing the elements and the enemy on watch became a preferred option to sharing the gloom in the wardroom. It was a situation which the unfortunate 'X' no doubt hoped to alleviate by coming round to each one of us singly and apologizing for the relatively minor damage he had done. He himself might have felt better after it, but the experience of another human being's moral degradation was distressing to the rest of us.

In retrospect one wonders if the Senior Officer ashore really believed that there was a case against 'X'. At all events, we were never advised of the outcome of any disciplinary action which may have taken place. Perhaps his expensive training was not to be wasted over such a trifling matter as our wine stocks. Years later he was still with the Navy.

SL147/MKS38

The next homeward convoy had drawn together three
escorted portions: TOWY, NARCISSUS and ORCHIS setting
out with the Gibraltar section at 2100 hours on 1 February,
assisted by the trawler NORTHERN FOAM; our old
comrade BURZA would also join us on 8 February. Three
French corvettes had taken the opportunity to visit Casablanca and came back with a portion from there. They joined
on the 2nd, at the same time as the Freetown section, whose
local escorts then went back into Gibraltar. The Commodore
was Vice-Admiral FA Marten RN (Rtd.) in SS STUYVESANT
and he had charge now of 81 ships, including 24 Tank
Landing Ships going home for the Normandy landings; by
a previous calculation it can be seen that the sea was filled
from horizon to horizon.

NARCISSUS and ORCHIS took on oil-fuel from the
tanker SS SAN TIRSO on getting into the Bay of Biscay; and
that same morning a Junkers 290 reconnaissance craft flew
across the front of the convoy. The Admiralty must have
assumed that we had been reported to a lurking patrol line
by the German Intelligence Service, because we were reinforced within 48 hours; the calibre of the reinforcements
gave some indication to us of the importance of the
resources we were protecting. We were now to be supported
by the most successful anti-submarine group in the Atlantic,
the 2nd Escort Group, led by the now renowned Captain F.
J. Walker RN in STARLING. He brought with him not just
one, but two, escort carriers, HMS ACTIVITY and HMS
NAIRANA and five other sloops. His principal task seems
to have been an anti-U-boat patrol in mid-Atlantic, which
involved going to the aid of any convoy which was within
range and appeared threatened. He had started his patrol
on 29 January and already, on 1 February, had sunk U-502
with an attack of his own invention called 'Operation
Plaster'. This involved two sloops, side by side, overtaking
a detected but submerged U-boat at slow speed. During the
course of this slow progress both sloops would drop over

30 depth-charges, each at variously deep settings.

On 8 February, whilst the convoy got out of his way to starboard, Walker took over the direction of a 'Creeping Attack', another innovative *pas de deux* in slow motion. WOODPECKER on this occasion moved ahead of her sister-ship without operating her Asdic, so that the U-boat was unaware that an attacking ship was approaching. The directing ship, STARLING, told WOODPECKER when to launch depth-charges when she gauged her position to be over that of the U-boat, whose range and depth was measured by the Asdic. Thus perished U-762. In the early morning of the next day, 9 February, HF/DF readings in the two Senior Officer ships, and in the rescue ship MELROSE ABBEY at the back of the convoy, gave such a accurate triangulation of a U-boat position that all the sloops set off in pursuit, whilst the convoy prudently altered course to port.

When underwater contact was obtained by the sloops' leader, the same 'creeping' procedure was performed with STARLING directing MAGPIE, but with the variant that the latter was told to use her forward-throwing weapon, the Hedgehog, whose bombs would explode only on contact. The immediate success meant the end of U-238. On that same day STARLING and WILD GOOSE had gone back to the trusty, if slightly expensive, 'Operation Plaster' in order to dispose of U-734.

Walker now had to replenish depth-charge stocks from another convoy. He left behind him a traumatized wolf-pack and an exhilarated close escort group. He was not yet finished, however: on the 12th February WILD GOOSE sank U-424 and on the 19th the sloops sank in a more orthodox manner U-264; the latter had the good sense to surface and abandon ship, so that the entire German crew of 51 was rescued.[4]

What was immediately apparent about Walker's slow-moving attacks was that it minimized the danger to the attacking escorts of the acoustic torpedo which a cornered submarine might use in its defence. As had soon been known after the introduction of the acoustic weapon in September 1943, a surface ship travelling at 17 knots or more was too fast for the torpedo to catch up, whereas one travelling at 7 knots or less did not make enough noise to attract it. Walker's creeping attacks were delivered at 5 knots and neither U-boat nor acoustic torpedo ever seemed to hear him coming. Commander Evans of B3 was naturally elated and redoubled his calls for an end to R/T silence when crossing the Bay of Biscay. For him and increasingly for many of his colleagues it now seemed that not only R/T chatter but even shadowing Luftwaffe reconnaissance would be working for us by homing U-boats to their destruction and should thus be welcomed![5] Long before Walker's record-breaking patrol ended, the convoy where he had delivered his most immediately beneficial blows on behalf of Britain's sea-trade was safely home. At 1945 hours on 11 February 1944 convoy SL147/MKS38 had reached 10°W and NARCISSUS was once again enjoined to lead away the Loch Ewe section.

OS69/KMS43

B3 Group picked up the subsequent southward-bound convoy (Cdre. Sir E. O. Cochrane in SS JONATHAN HOLT) well to the west of Ireland with a week of northern February weather to go. Admiralty signals steered us clear of known U-boat assemblies but, in any case, conditions were so foul that the enemy was less likely to bother us than would the sea. The by now settled combination of TOWY (Senior Officer), five corvettes, a rescue ship and a rescue tug was bolstered for the most critical part of the Bay of Biscay by two escort carriers, HMS NAIRANA and HMS ACTIVITY.

In near impossible conditions the latter two gallantly tried to fly off reconnaissance patrols and lost five aircraft for their pains, mainly through crash landings whilst the mother ship was pitching in the swell. NAIRANA lost 2 Swordfish, 1 Hurricane and a Fulmar during the trip, leaving her with

13 aircraft; whereas ACTIVITY lost a Wildcat, leaving her with only 6 on arrival in Gibraltar on 6 March. On he very next day, the arrival of an old comrade, the Polish destroyer BURZA, was signalled.[6]

A memorable anniversary in Gibraltar

The great Rock, standing at the entrance of the Mediter-ranean, had been the most traditional naval bastion of all the Atlantic termini which we visited. So it was with some surprise that we were to witness an alien farce, on this occasion, played out, moreover, in full public view.

The drama was avidly watched by B3 Group at the time, but its scenario as outlined by one of the players, Chief Engineer P. Perdraut on board FFS ROSELYS, is best expressed in his own words; any lack of clarity of expression must be put down to my translation into English [interesting French slang will be shown in these square brackets].

The full flavour of the event can best be appreciated if three factors are borne in mind: in the first place, no French-man ever forgot how and when Mussolini declared war on France; secondly, French culture demands that wine should be drunk at meals (indeed, the scurrilous rumour was put about the British ships that an ammunition magazine had to be replaced in each Free French corvette by a huge bottle to contain it); and thirdly, their Senior Officer, the Captain of ROSELYS, was a venerable and courteous man, thought to be well-connected and influential in French circles. The curtain rose a few days before the first anniversary of FFS ACONIT's epic sinking of two U-boats:

'If my memory serves me well,' wrote Monsieur Perdraut, 'B3 Group arrived at Gibraltar on 9 March 1944. The prospect of spending a few days at ease in the sunshine filled our hearts with joy and made us forget the mists and the hard knocks of the North Atlantic. Our delight was somewhat overcast when, on entering harbour, we noticed on the starboard side a magnificent Italian cruiser, as clean as a new penny, haughtily wearing the flag with its tobacco jar [French slang: *'pot à tabac'*] emblem.

We had to tell everyone that the Allies had signed an armistice with the Italians and that they, having changed sides, had become our allies and henceforth one could count upon them . . . It goes without saying that this hopefully convincing speech did not convince anyone and that old memories were coming to the surface . . .

Our three French corvettes accordingly tied up right inside the port. ROSELYS alongside the jetty and ACONIT outside her. At the front of the Group was our old friend BLITSKAVITSA[7] and others of B3 Group. From that first evening, several rumours about encounters on shore between Italians and members of B3 Group made the mess-decks and the wardrooms happy and everyone awaited the second evening to count the blows struck. The second evening passed, tension mounted and did not augur well for the end of the stay.

11 March arrived and to celebrate the anniversary Captain Le Millier ordered a double issue [Fr: *'attribuá la double'*] of the daily wine ration to the crew of ACONIT and I imagine that no-one baulked at this little extra to the midday menu. On board ROSELYS we finished our meal; it was about half-past one o'clock and chatting was well under way when a Lieutenant of the Royal Navy appeared in the wardroom doorway. After saluting politely, he spoke directly to Captain Kolb-Bernard, reproaching him for the unthinkable behaviour of French seamen who had boarded an Italian motor-boat etc., etc.

Astonished by this news, the Captain declared that he knew nothing of this event, that he would make enquiries and asked him to come back later. It was then learned that several sailors, irritated by a shiny, Italian-flag-flying motor-boat close by, which was going to deposit its 'tourists' at the harbour steps, had spoken of capturing it. No sooner said than done.

Using the ship's dinghy [Fr: *'Youyou'*], they had taken the motor-boat by storm, roughly handled the bowman, the cox'n [Fr: 'le bosco'; literally 'the hunchback'] and the equipment and had carried off the fine flag. I do not know the details of their master-stroke but it was enough to jerk the English [sic] Admiralty out of its customarily British restraint, it not being used to such treatment since the end of commerce raiding [Fr: 'guerre de course'] and since the privateers of St Malo and Dunkerque.

So the British officer came back to ROSELYS whose 'Skipper' [Fr: 'Pacha'!], the oldest officer in the highest rank, was held responsible for this resurgence of patriotism. The conversation quickened particularly when the Englishman passed the order for Kolb-Bernard to present his apologies to the Italian Admiral. Magnificently he replied that he would only discuss the matter further with a British officer of the same rank as his own. Disconcerted, the British Lieutenant left the ship.

Some time later a Lieutenant Commander arrived and he got the same reception. Kolb-Bernard told him that if the British Admiral had some remarks to make to him, he could do so himself, face to face, without going through an under-ling [Fr: 'sous-fifre'; lit. 'second fife-player']. Meanwhile the Italian flag had been recovered from a malodorous place, wrapped in a newspaper and handed to the Lieutenant Commander. The response was not long in coming. An order from the Admiralty required Captain Kolb-Bernard to present himself to the Flag Officer without further delay.

The interview seems to have been rather stormy. Our Captain, whilst deploring his crew's behaviour, refused point-blank to present his apologies to the Italian Admiral, saying that if anyone should apologize it should rather be the Italian Admiral to the French Captain for the stab in the back [Fr: 'le coup de Jarnac'] in 1940, when we were in total disarray.

I think that the Englishman was very annoyed at this reply. He summoned urgently the French military attaché with the Algiers government and asked him to pass the order for Kolb-Bernard to present his excuses to the Italian

Admiral. The military attaché, who was I think a four-ringed Captain but not a pukka Free Frenchman, must have wondered what sort of a wasps' nest he had fallen into. However, as the great diplomat which he showed himself to be, he replied that it was impossible for him to give such an order without referring to his government, seeing that the Provisional Government of Algiers had not signed the peace agreement with the Italians.

The British Admiral must have got into a towering rage because he immediately ordered the French corvettes to leave the port and to anchor outside in the roadsteads. When Kolb-Bernard got back on board and passed on this order, a current of rebellion seized us and I declared that, being at 24 hours notice for sailing, I had undertaken maintenance of the engines which would require at least that amount of time to complete. This was a splendid idea which formed the basis of a message to the Admiralty and earned us a visit from a British Engineer (a Lieutenant Commander) to verify my claim. In the meantime the necessary measures were taken to make the tale plausible. But the British Engineer arrived with a smile and said to me: 'I do not doubt that you have some maintenance in hand but I imagine that you could complete it in 12 hours. Split the difference, can't we?' In the face of this understanding attitude and above all his conspiratorial smile, I agreed. We would go at 5 a.m. the next day.

In the evening we received a few messages (which had been conveyed through the Admiralty network) coming from Allied ships more or less saying '[in English] Well done Frenchies. W'll [sic] keep on!' To contain the problem, the Admiralty cancelled night shore leave for the Italians, only allowing them into the town until 5 p.m. After that time the Allies had free access, but the desire for a dust-up had now gone. At dawn then the three corvettes left harbour, but the British had taken the precaution to forbid us from passing too close to the cruiser.[8] We anchored in the roads even if a little sheepishly, but at the hoisting of colours a few hours later, some yells coming from the harbour attracted our attention. The crew of the Italian cruiser, assembled on the ship's forecastle, were booing us. This earned the following message from Captain Kolb-Bernard:

[In English] 'If you don't want any more trouble, keep your allies, the Italians, quiet . . . Please.'

The final chapter of this saga came with the end of the next convoy trip. On arriving in Gibraltar an English officer, a [post-]Captain I think, came on board to advise our Captain that the Admiral whom we had known after the previous convoy and whose name I forget, had been replaced and had been recalled to England.'[9]

Even we British were slightly shocked at the apparently exuberant manner in which the Italians behaved themselves in what had been, until very recently, an enemy port: serried ranks of officers would be strolling along Main Street shouting 'Ciaou!' to ranks of friends coming the other way. The few British officers and ratings who could be spared from their ships would step aside in a puzzled fashion. In common with M. Perdraut and his friends, I can recall no signal from the Admiralty warning us of what awaited us in Gibraltar nor any instruction as to how the Italians should be treated. There had arrived, of course, more than just one cruiser: I still have photographs from that time of at least three submarines. The British response, to the somewhat surprising turn of events, was merely one of inactive surprise. Perhaps we were secretly glad that someone else was the butt of French indignation for a change. From an Italian point of view, perhaps their hearts had not been in the War from the start and they were now giving vent, in the safer presence of a more civilized Ally, to their relief at being out of it. As for the Parthian shot at the alleged 'Admiral', this was not, of course, the Flag Officer In-Charge (FOIC) Gibraltar, but his Chief of Staff; this was made clear later by an Appendix to a post-War history of the Free French Naval Forces.[10] This document also makes clear, a fact not evident to the rest of us at the time, the enduring resentment of the French towards her old ally, us, caused by this incident: they who had stood by us since the grim days of 1940 received little toleration, whereas those new 'chums', the Italians, had their indisciplined insults to the French colours at sunset overlooked. Perhaps on reflection the French could now see the incident in terms of a 'return of the prodigal son' complex: the dedication of the Free French to the prosecution of the War was beyond question: who knows what offended Italians might have done at that juncture?

Undoubtedly there was something unsympathetic about the great harbour of Gibraltar, unlike the other Atlantic termini. I now find the B3 Group was not the only escort group to upset the authorities there. In his long auto-biographical account of 5 years' continuous service at sea (unassisted by a diary?), Commander D. A. Rayner, RNVR, hardly ever has a bad word to say about anyone; but he did suffer a succession of mishaps in Gibraltar during the summer of 1944. As Senior Officer of B4 Group in HMS HIGHLANDER he recalls having been given 'one of the biggest "dressing downs" I have ever received'.[11] Raynor's major mishap was that, at a boisterous mixed party with the other ships' captains, some thunderflashes were thrown into the water from their motor-boat, causing the entire garrison of the Rock to go to action stations. Threatened with arrest, Rayner was glad to find, on the Group's return to the UK, that the C-in-C, Western Approaches, Admiral Horton, did not take any notice of that faraway fracas.

References

[1] Churchill, W. A., 1985, *The Second World War*, Vol. III, Guild Publishing, pp. 135–7.

[2] ADM 199/976.

[3] Rohwer & Hümmelchen, *op. cit.*, Vol. II, p. 377.

[4] Robertson, T., 1956, *Walker R. N.*, Evans Bros, pp. 164–78.

[5] ADM 199/315.

[6] ADM 237/883.

[7] M. Perdraut's memory after 50 years is remarkable: only 2 days

out over the arrival in port; but he must have been thinking of another old Polish comrade, ORP GARLAND, who had escorted the Russia-bound convoy PQ16 in May 1942 with ROSELYS (see B. B. Schofield, 1971, *The Russian Convoys*, Pan Books, p. 64). As we now know from the so-called 'pink list' – a highly secret document giving the daily location of all ships (locations from the 6th to 11th March 1944 are to be found in ADM 187/34) –, it was the Polish ORP BURZA who arrived in Gibraltar on 7th March; the same pink list tells us that ORP BLYSKAWICA was undergoing a refit on the Clyde on that date.

[8] The same pink list, again, names the Italian cruiser as the GUISEPPE GARIBALDI.

[9] Pierre Perdraut's account was published in the Flower Class Corvette Association's magazine, *Corvette Cracker*, translated into English, in 1996.

[10] Chaline, E. *Historique des F. N. F. L.*, pp. 453–4.

[11] Rayner, D. A., 1974, *Escort*, Futura, p. 203.

CHAPTER 11

A Taste of 'Tobermory' and
Farewell to B3 Group

After the Franco-Italian fracas we dutifully filed out of Gibraltar to escort, at an average forward speed of 8 knots, the 54 ships of the combined West African and Mediter- ranean convoys SL151/MKS42 on their last leg homewards. One more especially precious unit committed to our care on this occasion was the passenger liner, DUNNOTTAR CASTLE, carrying 2,749 personnel. Almost immediately we lost Commodore E. K. Boddam-Whetham, CBE, DSO, of the Mediterranean section, an old comrade of one of our previous October convoys, who had to be landed at Gibraltar with small-pox.[1]

We still had the Commodore of the West Africa section, however, Sir Charles Ramsey in SS SARPEDON. He was more successful than we had been in landing unwanted fellow-travellers: six stowaways from West Africa in one of his ships were promptly disembarked in Gibraltar; there the First Lieutenant, of the Navy ship which was to carry them back to their home, handed each one a paint-chipping hammer for the duration of their stay on board. This may not have been a very hospitable reception of those unfortunates who merely wanted to make better lives for themselves, but it was a much better fate than that which awaited, nearly fifty years later, similar stowaways on a Russian freighter off Africa: namely, to be dumped over the side of the ship.

The normal escort Group of TOWY, five corvettes and, on this occasion, two of our Polish regulars, BURZA and PIORUN, was enhanced by both a French 'guest', LA DECOUVERTE, and HMS COWSLIP. Our own 'constant companion', ORCHIS had recently acquired a new commanding officer, Lieutenant B. W. Harris, RNVR and, on this trip he was to discover the vagaries of the Hedgehog weapon: they did not experience such a drastic disaster with it as had our late friend, ESCAPADE, but they did find out that its projectiles might explode prematurely on contact with the surface of the water, instead of with the hull of a submarine.

There were several possible sightings of conning-towers during the passage and, for the last 150 sea-miles of the run into the relative safety of 7°30' West, the 7th Support Group screened the convoy from ahead. Apart from the hazard of oiling from a tame tanker, NARCISSUS really had not had a lot to do on this trip; whether he had got bored with inaction, or whether he had been tipped off by Flag Officer, Gibraltar, to have a go at us after the Italian fiasco of the previous visit, I do not know, but the Senior Officer decided to inspect us at sea! This was the day before we started to enjoy the luxury of cover by the 7th SG, so I suppose the safety of the convoy was in no doubt.

NARCISSUS is not the Senior Officer's favourite ship

We were aware that the Senior Officer viewed us with a somewhat jaundiced eye, because of an incident which had occurred in Lough Foyle off Londonderry in Northern Ireland soon after Commander Evans had taken over B3 Group. Ships of the Group were then anchored off Moville, but out of the Republic of Ireland's territorial waters. The Senior Officer's motor-boat, probably the apple of his eye, had been on some inter-ship message when its engine broke down and it began to drift westwards. After a while it became apparent that the motor-boat might soon go aground on the Irish coast and would then have been interned with its two-man crew. A distraught Senior Officer asked the new Captain of NARCISSUS, who had just been promoted from the command of a trawler, to rescue his craft, since we were closest to it and had steam up.

This we duly did, saving the boat from the shoals just in time and the crew from a couple of years of dalliance with rye whiskey and smiling Irish eyes. A working party attached the motor-boat to the port waist of the corvette by two ropes, stem and stern and we started to hasten back to the senior ship with a collective smile for a job well done.

I had the misfortune that day to be on watch, but the Captain rightly took over the con and, as an afterthought, told me to look over the wing of the bridge to see how the motor-boat was towing. What I then saw stunned even my inexperience: the haste of the corvette, to carry the Senior Officer's pride-and-joy back to him, was causing a bow-wave into which the motor-boat was crashing. As I opened my mouth to shout to the Captain, the tow-rope parted, the boat swung sideways, overturned and sank.

There was an immediate and almighty gefuffle about the two-man crew: no heads were bobbing in the Lough; it was going to be bad enough telling the Senior Officer that we had lost his precious motor-boat, but to have to tell him that we had drowned his sailors as well . . . ! As the port waist of the now stopped corvette filled with searching eyes, an unfamiliar Petty Officer asked what we were now looking for. 'The men in the boat!' everyone shouted.

'Well, I was the cox'n, and the motorman and I climbed out as soon as the boat was secured for and aft.' No-one had though to tell the bridge.

An inspection at sea

So on the 21st March 1944 it was with some misgiving that NARCISSUS received, whilst zigzagging in front of the convoy on an otherwise sunny day, an order from TOWY:

'Send your youngest officer and a sea-boat's crew to fetch the Senior Officer for a Ship's Inspection.' There were two 27-foot whalers, slung on davits either side of the funnel in a corvette. Their capacity was 16 men each and they were fitted out as lifeboats, but unlikely to be used as such: torpedoed or mined corvettes rarely had the time to launch boats. In consequence they were not often inspected; one recollected that, when NARCISSUS's previous First Lieutenant had inspected them after a dockyard refit in 1942, their emergency rations were found to have been looted.

The whaler selected for the task was swung outboard with some difficulty as, in the continual struggle against rust in any sea-going ship, the joints in the davits had been painted over. Lowering to sea-level was not a problem; fortunately, Commander Evans had chosen a calm day for his inspection, or perhaps he was not going to invest too much trust in our seamanship. As the seamen pulled the whaler across to the frigate, I noticed with growing alarm that water was rising within the boat.

As a well-polished pair of black Oxfords descended towards me down the frigate's rope ladder, I called up weakly: 'There's a bit of water in the boat, Sir.'

'I'm used to water, Sub.' came the unheeding reply, but when the first Oxford stepped into sea-water a foot deep, I could see that he was not pleased. We were still well ahead of the oncoming convoy and we managed to get the sodden boatload back to the corvette and hooked on to the davit falls before we were engulfed. Apart from a pause for the Senior Officer to change into a pair of borrowed shoes and socks, there was to be no respite; especially for me.

He decided that he would test the ship's gunnery next and I was the gunnery officer. In the early years of the War, convoys had been vexed by long-range enemy aircraft which circled convoys and reported their positions to U-boats. One response would be to provide one-time catapult Hurricane fighters to shoot down or at least to chase away such nuisances, but this was rather wasteful, because the fighter would have no deck to land back on; eventually, of course, this problem would be taken care of by escort aircraft carriers, as we have seen. Another antidote was to provide ships with anti-aircraft shells with very long fuzes reaching almost to the horizon and fired from the single 4-inch breech-loading gun carried by corvettes. So on this occasion the Senior Officer, standing at the back of the bridge, told me to have the gun's crew close up and fire at the empty horizon one round of high explosive, very-long-fuzed and it was to be supplied from the magazine.

If I had taken thought, I would have realized that he was merely trying to save time, testing the availability of the special shell as well as ensuring that we were capable of resupplying the gun on the upper deck with further supplies from the magazine in the bowels of the ship. Unfortunately, I had arranged to have all the few long-range shells stowed in ready-use lockers on the gun-deck and I did not have the heart to tell him that, so I miserably relayed his specifications down the voice tube to the gun captain.

This resourceful fellow was Petty Officer 'Knocker' White, the Chief Bosun's Mate and, over the spray-shield at the front of the bridge, I watched his reaction to this impossible order. True to every instinct in his being, he glanced up at the bridge ensuring that the Senior Officer could not see and took a round from a ready-use locker. I could then give the order to 'Shoot!' and fire was opened with commendable despatch.

'That was very good! Very quick too!' said the Senior Officer, 'Do it again.' And this time he came to the front of the bridge. P. O. White got his hands on another round from the ready-use locker as his eye met that of the Senior Officer, so he now recoiled and resignedly called for the round from the magazine. It came up reasonably quickly and the gun's crew performed as efficiently as they had done against U-260 but, unhappily, it turned out to be one of the shortest fuzed shells and, to my by now fevered perception, seemed scarcely to leave the barrel of the gun before exploding.

The firing of the close-range Oerlikon weapons passed

satisfactorily. I was spared on this occasion the embarrassment I suffered, at a later date, when the cheerful armaments artificer forgot to screw on fully the spare barrel of the 20mm Oerlikon, which he was testing informally; he saw it disappear into the sea with the first round fired. The shore-side gunnery supply officers were strict enough about accounting for and returning the brass shell cases of expended ammunition; their reaction to the explanation of an expended gun barrel is mercifully expunged from my memory.

Commander Evans went on to tease the signals branch with a request for 'jury', i.e. temporary replacement, aerials to be rigged. Where the ship's Captain really met his Nemesis however – and the rest of us nearly met our Maker – was in the Senior Officer's last scenario. The previous evolution had left us perilously close to the front rank of the convoy when, with a panache he seemed to have caught off Admiral Stephenson, the so-called 'Terror of Tobermory', he pronounced that the ship's main steering had broken down and we should go into 'hand steering'.

All modern ships have a small steering-wheel within the bridge structure, which, of course, is normally towards the bows of the ship. At cruising stations this wheel was normally manned by a rota of quartermasters, or the coxswain at action stations; its movements were transmitted mechanically to the rudder at the back of the ship. In a corvette at any rate, – I cannot answer for larger ships – there was also a massive steering wheel for emergency purposes sited directly under the depth-charge rails and over the rudder in a covered steering compartment, known to us as 'the tiller flat'. The only means of communication, between the Captain, on the bridge directing the course to be steered from the front of the ship, and the three men needed on this huge wheel with ten hand-holds, at the back of the ship, was by voicepipe.

It should have been a relatively simple matter for the Captain, in a 'hand steering' situation to shout his directions, 'Port Twenty!', 'Hard-a-Starboard!' etc, down the voicepipe and for an officer in the steering compartment in the stern to relay the order to the men on the emergency wheel.

On this occasion, or so it was claimed afterwards, dockyard engineers at the previous refit had re-assembled a stripped down emergency wheel in reverse. When the Captain of NARCISSUS tried to slip between the columns of the advancing, and somewhat bemused, convoy by ordering 'Starboard Ten' (i.e. turning the ship continuously ten degrees to starboard), the emergency wheel linkage with the rudder reversed this into 'Port Ten'; when the alarmed order, which then quickly followed, was 'Hard-a-Starboard!', the rudder put on 'Hard-a-Port'. After a great deal of bad language down the voicepipe it was realized that it was more important to save the whole ship than to continue testing parts of it and we returned quickly to main steering.

After these shattering experiences, it was a relief for all concerned, but especially for me, to discover that the Senior Officer had called over his own boat to take him away. More surprisingly, we never heard any more about it. The public Admiralty records of the event are disappointingly tight-lipped:

'[B.3] Senior Officer's Report.

Section 8 . . . Special Exercises at Sea

On 21st March I transferred first to NARCISSUS and later to RENONCULE for the purpose of carrying out a sea inspection of these ships. All the armament was exercised and various evolutions were carried out.'[2]

There is little doubt that these traumata experienced by the ship, recalled more enjoyably countless times later, stimulated more efficiency than any subsequent recrimination from shore officials might have done. Indeed there may have been almost a cult of what goes by the acronym of GNFU: quite apart from the relief these events provided from the sometimes excruciating monotony of routine, the occasional exception from clockwork smoothness proved its rule.

The fate of HMS ASPHODEL

On the other hand, there may have been a more serious cause for this unexpected, but evidently much required, retraining exercise. One month before, during the passage of a preceding northbound convoy, SL150/MKS41, a tragic event had occurred which showed that the acoustic torpedo, which we had been the first Group to encounter, was far from mastered despite the well deployed counter-measures. If so, however, it is odd that our 'evolutions' did not reflect the conclusions of the Court of Inquiry into the sinking of the corvette HMS ASPHODEL which were dated 9th March 1944.[3]

On the night of 9 February 1944 the veteran U-boat U-575, active in the North Atlantic since 1941,[4] was detected on the surface by ASPHODEL, who illuminated it with rocket-flares. The corvette captain had turned towards and had reduced speed to seven knots with Foxers streamed; so far, so good. But the U-boat, instead of diving, headed straight for the corvette. This provocative action caused the captain to order the Foxers to be made inoperative ('tripped'), enabling the corvette to charge at full speed (15 knots).

This was deemed by the Court of Inquiry to have been a mistake, for the U-boat had fired an acoustic torpedo as it came on. But the corvette captain was placed in a clear quandary: if he maintained slow headway against a charging U-boat, he was as likely to be sunk by ramming as the other way about. In the event, the torpedo struck and perhaps 70% of the crew managed to abandon ship; but worse was to follow. The corvette's depth-charges were primed to explode at a depth of 100 feet. When she sank the charges killed most of her own crew who were still on the surface; three survived to give evidence to the Court.[5]

This would be something of a digression from an account which tends to concentrate on the experiences of units of B3 Group and of HMS NARCISSUS, if it were not for three particulars. The first concerns the danger to an attacking escort of its own weapons: the fate of most of ASPHODEL's survivors forcibly reminded me of the arrival on board NARCISSUS of a Leading Torpedoman in 1943; he was a survivor from a destroyer sunk in a Russian convoy and had been decorated. His feat of gallantry had been to swim round the slowly sinking destroyer's after deck and withdraw the depth-setting keys from the depth-charges; this effectively neutralized them and saved the destroyer's survivors from what would now be termed 'friendly fire'.

The second lesson from ASPHODEL, as from escorts like GLADIOLUS and POLYANTHUS before her, was that warships, singly on the surface, had only a 50% chance of survival against submarines. Thirdly, awareness of the acoustic torpedo was no guarantee of immunity: ships continued to be sunk by them and the outcome of the Battle was not a foregone conclusion after May 1943, as some historians appear to have supposed. As for U-575, its progress was stopped soon afterwards by none other than USS BOGUE, the start of whose own career, with us in March 1943, had been less than auspicious.

The next Gibraltar-bound convoy, OS73/KMS47, gave some indication of the changing focus of the Battle: although it contained many ships bound southwards, 52 in 14 columns, it was not threatened by the enemy and suffered only stragglers.[6]

SL155/MKS46 and the end of an era

This homeward-bound convoy also foreshadowed the coming cross-Channel assault, including in its columns at least 11 Landing Ships (Tanks) and 29 Landing Ships (Infantry) all destined for Normandy. The Commodore was J. K. Brooke, CBE, DSO, RNR and B3 Group was enlarged with the presence of one of the new Castle Class corvettes, LEEDS CASTLE, and of various other escort ships 'hitching a ride', so to speak. The Castle Class was an augury of the future shape of southbound convoys to come, for the next mention of TOWY in the record would be of her in charge of a group of Castle Class corvettes alone.

Again, only the rescue ship, BURY, was actively engaged, running around chivying ships out of station and handing out medical advice to those ships carrying passengers. As the convoy passed close to the Spanish coast, searchlights lit up its starboard wing column. During the preceding winter this discovery might well have been followed by a gathering of predators, but not now. Indeed, air cover now seemed to be dispensed with and the Senior Officer felt he had to provide his own dummy enemy signals for an H/F, D/F exercise. 'necessary now that co-operation by U-boats is so sadly lacking.'

His experience with NARCISSUS on the previous northbound passage appears not to have dampened his enthusiasm for exercises, putting his own ship through them shortly after leaving Gibraltar. TOWY carried out a full-calibre shoot and practised the Hedgehog. It would be permissible to surmise, I think, that the conclusions of the Court of Inquiry into the loss of ASPHODEL had reached him by now, because he also had the Foxers streamed and exercised 'Abandon Ship!'. The Carley rafts took so long to pick out of the sea again, however, that he decided not to inflict that exercise upon the rest of us. To show that he could wag his tail as well as bite, the Senior Officer recorded a rather affecting little valedication in his final report, which I reproduce verbatim:

'This convoy provided the final escort duty of the old B.3 Group which, in its tri-allied form, has fought the Battle of the Atlantic almost since the fall of France.

If we were not all confident that the closing of this chapter is only the prelude to the opening of a new and even more gloriously offensive one, it would be a really sad moment. As it is, we say a cheerful 'Goodbye and Good Luck' to our many Polish and French friends whose faith, courage and enthusiasm have been an example to us and who have, by their unstinted loyalty, shown how three widely different nationalities can work together as one individual unit.'[7]

This message will have gone far towards healing the bitterness and the frustrations of our Allies in the early years. Commander Evans repaid with interest the trust that had been placed in him. He was rewarded for his good services with the post of Training Captain to the C-in-C Western Approaches.[8] On the 29th April 1944, 6 merchantmen, 11 Landing Ships (T) and 29 Landing Craft (I) left the convoy, escorted by the new frigate ANGUILLA, the 'guest' corvette ANCHUSA and NARCISSUS for the Bristol Channel. Farewell B.3.

References

[1] ADM 237/1226.
[2] ADM 199/318.
[3] *Ibid*.
[4] Rohwer & Hümmelchen, *op. cit.*, Vol. II, pp. 395, 594.
[5] ADM 199/318.
[6] ADM 217/71, ADM 237/887.
[7] ADM 199/318.
[8] W. S. Chalmers, 1954, *Max Horton and the Western Approaches*, Hodder & Stoughton, p. 208.

HMCS IROQUOIS.

*Plum O'Reilly, our South African
Engineer, with an Australian
passenger in the background.*

The second Captain, with the 2 Engineer officers and an RAF passenger from Gibraltar in 1944.

Formal portrait of the crew, 1944 (note the square HF/DF receiver aerial.)

Formal portrait of the officers, 1944: (note the rocket-flare rails, added to the 4" gun shield after September 1943).

CHAPTER 12

The last act: Normandy

Most of May 1944 was taken up with rest, recreation and repairs at the tiny port of Troon in Ayrshire, where we lorded it as the 'big ship in the harbour', an unusual status for us. We did not, of course, neglect the necessary re-training for our future role in the assault on Europe. Having been told to emphasize air defence rather than anti-submarine warfare, those who were not on long leave were transported from time to time to the nearest anti-aircraft training dome.

The shape of things to come was revealed to us with the arrival alongside of two Landing Craft (Gun); in a parody of the famous ribaldry, some ships have big guns and some are 'all gun'. These craft were of the latter type: a tiny vessel, designed to disembark 30 infantrymen, had been converted to carry a 4-inch breach-loader; a gun which looked big even on our own somewhat larger forecastle. These LC(G)s were intended to beach opposite some German fortification and blast away at it until following troops could land under this covering fire. The two of them were commanded by Royal Marines Lieutenants, who both happened to be South Africans. This was the first time I had seen Royal Marines in the Western Approaches and was evidently dazzled by them.

The two craft lay alongside NARCISSUS and, partly because our own Engineer Sub/Lieutenant 'Plum' O'Reilly was also a South African, there was a great deal of mutual entertainment. Unhappily, both craft were lost in the Royal Marines operation to capture the island of Walcheren, in the

183

mouth of the Scheldt, the following November.

Towards the end of the month we were ordered to proceed independently to an invasion port, but the long way round, northabout through the Pentland Firth. This we accomplished in seemingly leisurely fashion, stopping at Methil in Fifeshire to refuel. This route enabled us to experience the conditions under which the east coast convoys had frequently had to be defended against German E-boats: the constant changes of course; the calm coastal seas so propitious to fast torpedo-boat attack; the eerie silences of these misty waters.

One hilarious anecdote from this period enlivened what was otherwise a rather dull passage. It concerned an escort vessel trying to enter one of the small harbours on this northeastern coast of Scotland and getting herself stuck on a sandbar. Much bad language had to flow and many hours had to be spent waiting for the high tide to float her off. When she did so, her captain, the bearer of a famous name, in his frustration forgot to say 'Hard a'starboard!', before he said 'Full speed ahead!' He inevitably went straight back on to the sandbank for another twelve hours.

NARCISSUS finally came to Sheerness, on the island of Sheppey in the mouth of the Thames. Accustomed as we had been to large and combined convoys in the latter part of the Atlantic Battle, they were dwarfed by this aggregation of hundreds of vessels of all categories and sizes which now presented themselves to view. A few were still embarking men and weapons, but most were at anchor and 'loaded to the gunwales', or so they seemed.

Only two events stay in my memory from that wait at Sheerness. One was the overflight of the Thames Estuary in daylight of a multi-bomber raid by United States' Flying Fortresses, heading for Germany in close formation for mutual defence. Just as they were above us, two bombers touched wings and broke up; from one I counted eight parachutes descending into the water, quickly to be approached by some of the many lighters and tenders buzzing to and fro.

The other memory was of the ease with which one could move about. Most of my leaves of absence from the ship in Scotland, after a rather laborious train journey, had been spent in the West End, but based at my aunt's house at Yiewsley near London. Now, at the beginning of June 1944, it seemed rather dashing to see her directly from the ship and to tell her conspiratorially 'This is IT!' On a day when I was not required on board I arranged to meet her and my uncle at a bar in Paddington station. I was rather surprised and perhaps slightly dismayed not to be turned back at Sheerness station. Of course the Germans knew something was coming, but they did not know exactly when and where; any more than I did until we were heading down the Channel. Yet, and in retrospect, I am amazed that there was not a firmer imposition of security.

'D'-Day

The 'Follow Up' and 'Build Up' of the eastern Assault Force upon Normandy (British and Canadian armies) were going to come from out of the Thames Estuary and Essex. The Follow up Force was denominated 'Force L' and comprised 5 groups, each escorted by a destroyer and one to two corvettes. Waiting between Sheerness and Southend, besides NARCISSUS, were the corvettes CAMELIA, CHARLOCK, CLEMATIS, BORAGE, GODETIA, MIGNONETTE, OXLIP and LOOSESTRIFE.

NARCISSUS's sailing group was 'L1', comprising the 7th and 8th Landing Ship (Tank) Flotillas; each LS(T) was reportedly capable of transporting 8 jeeps, 21 3-ton lorries, 6 15-cwt. lorries and 18 tanks, together with 177 men.[1] Convoy L1 consisted of 11 such Landing Ships and 8 Landing Craft (Infantry). The plan was for the LSTs to carry the 3rd Canadian Division to Juno beach and for the LCIs to carry the 51st [Highland] Division to Gold beach. The Senior Officer of the escorts was Lieutenant Commander J. W. Whittle, DSC, RNVR, in the Hunt-class destroyer

COTSWOLD, with NARCISSUS, OXLIP and the trawler DAMSAY.

The departure times for all the Force L groups was linked to the time of the first beach assault in France, 'H' Hour. Thus our sailing time from the Thames Estuary was 'H' minus 22 hours; L1 convoy was timed to arrive at the northern end of the swept channel through the suspected German minefield at H minus 1½ hours. The calculated speed for the passage between the Thames and the entry of the swept channel was 8 knots. I have no recollection of being turned around when 'D'-Day was delayed by 24 hours in 1944, as happened to at least one of the assault convoys, so 'D'-Day and 'H'-Hour must have been postponed before we were due to start out.

The convoy started out in single file with the escorts between their charges and the enemy coast. On arrival at the Sandhead Buoy outside Dover, the convoy opened out into four columns with the large LSTs in two inner columns flanked by one of the smaller LCI columns on either side.

It was during this period, of changeover to the westward leg of our measured approach towards the Isle of Wight, that we made a fortuitous change of course, when I was on watch. NARCISSUS was on the port, i.e. seaward, side of the convoy when I noticed that we had drifted away from the nearest LST. Altering course twice, once to close the nearest column and then to turn parallel to the original course, I was startled on regaining station to see an enormous spout of water rise where NARCISSUS would have been if she had not moved closer to the convoy.

The first speculation of everyone on the bridge was that an acoustic or a magnetic mine had somehow been triggered off; but there was none of the roar that one was accustomed to hear from an underwater explosion, either a mine, a torpedo, or a depth-charge. Although we were by then south of Dover, our eventual conclusion was that a German coastal battery on the French side of the Channel had ranged on us but, by the time the shell had laboriously winged its way to us, we had moved two or three hundred yards 'sideways'!

At K1 Buoy, south of Portsmouth, Convoy L1 formed into two columns with the LSTs leading. Here we were joined by Motor Minesweeping Flotilla no. 143 and by several coasters. We were also joined by a Landing Ship so especially valuable that, on arrival at the Normandy beaches, it was to be escorted personally to a specified discharging position, where its amphibious craft (DUKWs) would 'swim' off. This vessel was carrying the Army and Army Group Staffs for Juno beach[2]; Montgomery himself, of course, would rejoin them within 24 hours, after a rather swifter passage in HMS FAULKNOR.

At the entrance to the swept channel no. 7, at Latitude 50°05' North, the whole of Convoy L1 turned on to a course of 160° and proceeded at 6¼ knots in single file for 8.4 miles; then on a course of 177° for 24.7 miles to a position, where the LSTs would lower their assault craft, at 49°27'24"N 0°27'00"W precisely.

Most of the southward leg of the approach was steamed during the middle and morning watches of 'D'-Day, of course, for our follow-up wave of tanks and troops was due to catch the second tide of the day. By now all the ships had streamed anti-aircraft balloons. The entrance to the channel through the German minefield was guarded by a Motor Launch (commanded by an ace navigator, I should not wonder, for it would have been in his power to run the entire operation into the minefield!) flying flag no. 7. Every mile of the swept channel was marked by buoys which, in the case of channel no. 7, flashed twice every six seconds.

Despite meticulous instructions as to how to dispose of floating mines, which were expected to be dropped by German planes into the swept channels, we saw none. We were visited by one enemy aircraft, during that morning of D-Day as we filed slowly but inexorably southwards between the minefields: it weaved its way through the balloons and the hearty anti-aircraft fire. We assumed it was on a reconnaissance mission, counting the ships. We also saw one airman, nationality unknown, drifting along in his life-jacket face downwards. Even if he had been within the swept channel, no-one would have stopped to pick him up: the operation orders specified quite clearly that no ship was to leave the swept channel and that nothing was to delay the follow-up.

Back in the Straits of Dover, at noon on that same D-Day, a freighter in the first of the 'Build Up' convoys from the Thames, ETM1, and carrying troops and their vehicles for Juno beach, the Liberty-type SAMBUT, suffered the fate that had nearly befallen us: she was struck by two German shells, was set on fire and sank.[3]

Normandy

The scene on the afternoon of 'D'-Day, 9 hours after 'H' Hour, was more than memorable; as the LSTs began to disgorge their passengers and the special Army headquarters ship was ushered away, we had time to look around. Half a mile to the East the 15-inch guns of the battleship WARSPITE ('big ship, big guns') and the monitor ROBERTS ('small ship, all gun') were banging away at targets on shore; whereas the beaches around Arromanches and Courseulles looked merely busy, with landing craft of all sizes hastening towards them, to the West beyond Port-en-Bessin, smoke covered the beaches and bullets and shells were flying about. This was the near disaster of Omaha beach, where the American assault troops were having difficulty getting out of the water.

Our southward duty done, we now reported to the rather grandly named Captain of the Northbound Sailing flying flag 9. He was a traffic controller stationed at the southern end of the swept channel and he required us, with OXLIP, to escort Convoy FTL1 back to Sheerness. A whole new series of convoy acronyms was invented for the assault and build-up. This first return convoy from France to the Thames, for example, was named for 'country of departure', 'area of arrival' and 'contents' ('L' for LSTs).

In the meantime our sister corvettes were not far behind

The graves of 2 ORCHIS casualties at Ryes Military Cemetery in Normandy.

us: MIGNONETTE with L2 left at 'H' hour minus 21 hours; GODETIA and CLEMATIS with L3 at H – 16½; BORAGE and LOOSESTRIFE with L4 at H – 16; CAMELIA and CHARLOCK with L5 at H – 5. NARCISSUS returned to Sheerness and by 8 June had started back, on what was to become an almost continuous shuttle service, escorting ETM5 ('England/Thames, Motor Transport') to the beachhead.

My time with NARCISSUS was now up and, since I had responded to an appeal in Admiralty Fleet Orders for officers to transfer to the Royal Marines, I reported to the RM Barracks at Chatham early in August. By doing so I missed our sister ship, ORCHIS's, hours of glory. On the 15th August, whilst in charge of the returning convoy FTC68, she sank U-741 in 50°02'N 00°36'W with her Hedgehog weapon. Three Germans surfaced, of whom one survived to be picked up by her. Within 15 days ORCHIS was herself torpedoed close to the beaches, happily with few lives lost.

Once the first frantic months of re-supply to the beaches were over, NARCISSUS was released from that work. For the last three months of 1944 and until the war in Europe was over, she was employed as a local escort for ships which were now able to use, with relative impunity, the South-Western Approaches.

This role was a pale shadow of the one she had first assumed in the more dangerous days of 1941. Now based at Plymouth, her task was to meet incoming convoys from Freetown and/or Gibraltar in a position southwest of the Scilly Isles. Together with one or more consorts, she would usher them eastwards to the Solent or even to the Downs. Thus, for example, would she service convoys MKS64/SL173 in October 1944, MKS76 in January and MKS97 in May 1945.

Similarly, NARCISSUS would customarily help to shepherd the English Channel contributions to outward-bound composite convoys, which had started out from the Clyde, picking up Belfast and Liverpool and Milford Haven sections, on a stately progress down through the Irish Sea. Thus, for example, the Canadian escort group, C4, collected the Clyde and Belfast sections of ON268 off Mew Island on 24 November 1944 and, on emerging from the southern end of the Irish Sea, were joined by the Channel section, conducted thither on the 26th by NARCISSUS and two others. The Channel local escorts only stayed a day before returning to Plymouth.

Likewise, the triple convoy OS125/KMS99/ON299, starting from Liverpool, by 27 April 1945 had the confidence to process down the Irish Sea with ON299 one mile in front, instead of on a broad front as had been the North Atlantic practice. On the 29th the Channel section joined this gathering on its easterly course and, at midnight, the southbound OS and KMS convoys 'wheeled' 90° to port, detaching themselves thereby from the northbound ON convoy. The very next day all but one of the warships left to escort in MKS97 and, on 1 May, the convoy dispersed in 44°26'N, 10°00'W, only HMS OXFORD CASTLE continuing with them to Gibraltar.

It is clear that, by this time, the escort groups had become not only somewhat heterogeneous but also rather loosely integrated; not everyone liked the comings and goings. The Captain of LEEDS CASTLE, for example, complained of the consequent overload of work for a Senior Officer: his composite convoy '. . . has ships joining and leaving all the time, most of whom he does not know personally.' Group continuity and the benefits of a team spirit must, however, have seemed less paramount, now that the European war was nearly over.

In the meantime, NARCISSUS's old group continued to beat against the elements. It now comprised a more variegated selection of escort vessels: in 1945 B3 was led by EXE, a River-class frigate; the Group now contained a Captain-class frigate, GARDINER, a Castle-class corvette and one 'exotic', GERANIUM.

The captain of one of them had been the first Captain of NARCISSUS, promoted now, decorated, but still the victim of the odd mishap. In April 1945 in Convoy ONS47, a fireman from a merchantship had been treated for three days by the Master for 'fireman's cramp', but became so ill that he had to be taken on to the warship at sea. When he was looked at, it was clear that the unfortunate man had peritonitis and soon died.

The same warship also lost its 'Unifoxer' (the anti-acoustic defence vibrator) to an unexplained explosion. Poor Captain, I expect he still appeared to be nursing a secret sorrow, there had been no respite for him. His experience seems to have been typical in a nation which contributed more than its fair share to a global conflict: as far as the professional Navy was concerned, its small pool of experts had to keep on giving to the limit in order for the cause of the Allied nations to stay afloat.

For NARCISSUS the only relief from eight months of jobbing duties, delivering and collecting small parcels of ships to and from 38 convoys, seems to have been involvement in an enemy attack on Granville between 9 and 18 March 1945. Perhaps it was on the return journey from this task, off Guernsey in calm waters, that an old lady dressed in black was observed rowing a small boat; when asked in French if she required any assistance she apparently waved it away, replying angrily that she was making for England![4]

On 21 May NARCISSUS escorted six surrendered German Minesweepers from Plymouth to Brest. On 25 May she was ordered to Milford Haven to de-ammunition, Before being laid up in Reserve Category C, NARCISSUS sailed up the river Ribble to Preston, from where the ship's crew took transport to Denton, a town southeast of Manchester which had adopted the ship during the War. There the crew thanked the townspeople for the many 'comforts' (books, socks, etc.) provided over the years and were royally entertained by them.[5] On 5 April 1946 she was sold as SS ESTE, later renamed PLANETA. On 27th June 1969 she was wrecked off Bahia in the South Atlantic.

It is pleasing to record that the wartime service of the first leader of B3 Ocean Escort Group ended on a more upbeat note: the day after peace was declared in Europe a destroyer arrived in the Channel Islands to accept the surrender of the German garrison there: that destroyer was HMS BULLDOG. It had been she who had delivered a decisive intelligence blow at the enemy in 1941, with the capture of U-110's Enigma decyphering machine; now she had survived until 1945 to accept that enemy's final surrender.

References

[1] John de S. Winser, 1994, *The D-Day Ships,* World Ship Society, p. 90.
[2] ADM 199/1560, pp. 112–113, 132. It must be appreciated that for the greater part of the background narrative, from 1941 to May 1944 dealing with the long trans-Atlantic convoys, I have relied upon *subsequent* Admiralty records; whereas for the short cross-Channel convoys, of June 1944, I have had to rely upon the *preceding* operational orders for Operation 'Neptune'. I believe that this prospective approach to events turns out to be as justified as the retrospective method because, despite the unfavourable weather,

historians agree that the plan, on D-Day at least, was carried out *to the letter*, e.g. Correlli Barnett, *op. cit.*, p. 825. It has to be said that some differences of detail do appear: for example, the LST numbers I have given are those in the operational orders, but Winser (p. 91) does add 9 United States LSTs to Convoy L1, arriving in the Eastern Task Force area on 6th June.

[3] Winser, *op. cit.*, p. 55.

[4] Personal communication on 15 Jan 1994 from Alwyn Davies, ex-stoker in NARCISSUS.

[5] Personal communication on 20 Dec 1994 from Gordon Drew, ex-navigator in NARCISSUS.

Unpublished sources for this chapter are: ADM 199, /317, /319, /498, /1620; 217/140; 237/431; and Ruegg, *op. cit.*, p. 6.

Conclusions

The Ship

HMS NARCISSUS was not destined to be an heroic ship: she shot down no planes and sank no U-boats; indeed, as far as I am aware, her crew only ever saw two conning-towers, although the first one was dealt with effectively. It is with good reason that ships are treated as living beings and not as inanimates; for, apart from the collective spirit that they are perceived to inspire, they may wax and wane like any living thing.

NARCISSUS and her crew had come green to the Battle in 1941 and undertook initially the minor task of local escort. In the more perilous years of 1942 and 1943 she blossomed, together with her consorts. She and her sisters stood at the centre of the Battle, fighting as part of a systematic and co-ordinated campaign, fending off both the elements and a persistent enemy; in reality, of course, she was mainly holding the lifeline until more sophisticated rescuers could emerge. In these middle years the major struggle was in mid-Ocean, where the plain confrontation between surface and sub-surface warriors was as yet hardly affected by the airpower of either side. With the end of the mid-Ocean phase, the Flower-class corvette became just one more type of escort vessel, merged with growing numbers of sloops, frigates and other classes of corvette.

Loss of central position was delayed by the climactic assault on Europe but, once the Normandy beachhead was secure, the Flower-class corvette shared the fate of the ex-American destroyer and the ocean-going trawler before her: now she would be demoted to the subsidiary role of local escort, ushering and delivering parcels of ships to the big boys, the River-class and Captain-class frigates; it was they now who left shallow waters for the ocean.

The ultimate indignity for a fighting ship, or the ultimate tribute to her sea-keeping qualities, whichever way one wishes to look at it, lay in NARCISSUS's translation into a commercial vessel. Like the classic old soldier she was, she took her pay and faded away.

The Clyde Escort Force

In the 'pink lists' of 1941 this Force appeared to be a rather motley collection of elderly destroyers, untried corvettes and unallocated French and Polish vessels whose capacity and commitment may have seemed unclear to Their Lordships in those early days. Unknown to all but a few, however, two of their number had already struck a blow for Britain which must count among the turning points, not just of the Battle but, of the whole War: in May HMS BULLDOG and HMS AUBRETIA carried out together an Operation (outlined in chapter 3) which would help to lead the German nation down the 'Primrose' (as the operation was rather aptly called) path to destruction.

The makeshift and essentially uneconomic short-haul escorting of 1941 was overtaken by the changed strategic conditions which prevailed post-'Barbarossa' and post-Pearl harbour: one new Ally would need bolstering with war materials taken by sea to Murmansk; the other Ally could now give overt support and, more especially, make ship-servicing facilities available on the westward seaboard of the Atlantic. Thus the short-haul groups EG3 and EG4 of the Clyde Escort Force would henceforth lose their old 'A' and 'B' class destroyers, some corvettes and a Polish destroyer to the Russian run; lose an ex-American four-stacker to the Newfoundland Force; and lose some corvettes to the Londonderry Force.

Those who remained would constitute the new B3 Ocean Escort Force from 24 February 1942; they would soon be joined, as Senior Officer's ship by the new 'H' class destroyer, HARVESTER, currently refitting at Dundee. The ploy now would be to escort convoys all the way across the Atlantic, enabling Royal Navy ships to establish a closer rapport with the merchant ships they were protecting, as well as strengthening ties and developing anti-submarine tactics with each other.

Despite the low points of March and September 1943, when the HARVESTER and ITCHEN were lost, the new long-haul strategy bore down upon the enemy to a point where he was no longer to be avoided but was increasingly to be challenged. Quite apart from participating in and contributing to the U-boats' retreat from the North Atlantic during the summer of 1943, B3 Group showed, by early in 1944 on its new route across the Bay of Biscay, an inclination to attract the attentions of the 'wolf pack' rather than to avoid them.

The B3 Group of 1943/43 was characterized by defiance and cavalier nonchalance; the B3 Group of 1943/44 was tinged with gritty professionalism, with a touch of triumphalism even. By mid-1944 the classic B3 team of British, French and Polish escort ships had reached a high degree of mutual understanding and individual confidence. Paradoxically but inevitably, now was the moment for the ships of the old Groups to be dispersed to other tasks and to be replaced by homogeneous groups of Castle-class corvettes or Captain-class frigates. The crews in these later groups had, of course, in large part learned their trade in the Flowers, as we have seen with the first captain of the NARCISSUS. So that no fighting skill was lost in the process of technological modernization.

Before we leave B3 Group, it is appropriate to recall the

fates of its early leaders. BOADICEA had unhappily been sunk by aircraft off the Normandy beaches in June 1944, but BULLDOG and BEAGLE survived to convey the British representatives who received the German surrender of the Channel Islands on May 8th 1945; also there in Operation 'Nestegg' was our Polish comrade ORP GARLAND.

IN MEMORIAM

"THEIR NAME LIVETH FOR EVERMORE"

HMS BOADECIA.—Sank June 13, 1944. We remember those who served.
H.M.S. BOADICEA.—Remembering with pride and affection the 176 Officers and Ratings lost in action in H.M.S. Boadicea, June 13, 1944.
VAUGHAN.—MALCOLM, Flt. Lt. R.A.F. Died June 13, 1986 in a parachuting accident. Since joined by his father, DENNIS, 3 Para. (Retired). Memories cherished by their loving family.

The Battle

Although the Royal Navy had anticipated the need for large numbers of convoy escort vessels even before war broke out, the criteria for those that were ordered could not be expected to match the task they were eventually called upon to perform. Whereas the short-forecastled corvette was equal to its sea-keeping duties, its speed and endurance were not. The latter quality was able to be modified in time, but the former had to await the appearance of a new class, the Castles, whose twin-screwed engines raised their speed to above the critical mark of 17 knots.

Another strategic problem raised by the occupation of French west coast ports by the German U-boats was the mid-Ocean gap, which predatory submarines could now reach but protective, land-based aircraft could not. This was gradually resolved by, first of all C(atapult) AM ships, then MAC ships and finally by escort carriers.

The third strategic problem was that of scarce resources: escort ships could not both remain with their convoys and hunt U-boats to destruction; the solution had to await the arrival of separable 'killer' groups, like Walker's sloops of EG2. The remaining problems were mainly technological or tactical, the answers to which were worked out, either by scientists and engineers in Britain, or by sailors in tactical units or on the high seas. Pride of place must, I think, go to the extraordinary achievements of the code-breakers at Bletchley Park for providing frequent and timely warning of U-boat dispositions. To them must go the credit for the early avoidance of U-boat concentration. Also as each difficulty presented itself at sea, some 'boffin' at home came up with a counter-measure, whether it was a forward-firing Hedgehog, a Leigh-light for aircraft to see surfaced U-boats at night, or a towed rattle to divert acoustic torpedoes.

Tactical advances were made, particularly after contact with an underwater enemy had been achieved. Perhaps the principal one was Walker's 'creeping attack', which took away from evasive U-boat captains the option of last-minute avoidance.

The greatest factor in the Battle, however, in my opinion, was the ordinary and able seaman's unfailing patience and quirky humour in the foulest and often least hopeful conditions. The enemy was brave and usually paid an horrendous price for his temerity in trying to reach and cut our ship-borne lifeline, but there was never any question of his prevailing against the oaken hearts which barred his way.

On the other hand the abiding legacy, of the series of events portrayed here, is a recognition of the awe-inspiring responsibility of operational command. If there is a paramount lesson to be learned from both triumph and tragedy, it is that no amount of training can guarantee that swift decisions, required from leaders, will be cost-free.

Admiral Horton, Commander Evans, Lt. Cdr. Levasseur of ACONIT and Cdr. Kolb-Bernard of ROSELYS.

Horton with Captain Roberts and Commander Evans.

Post-War reunion of B3 Group with shore-based guests, 1946/7.

Bibliography

All the World's Fighting Ships, 1922–1946, Conway, 1980.

Barnett, C. *Engage the Enemy More Closely*, Hodder & Stoughton, 1991.

Brown, D. K., *The Design and Construction of British Warships, 1939–1945*, Vol. II, Conway, 1996.

Chaline, E. *Historique des F.N.F.L.*

Chalmers, W. S., *Max Horton and the Western Approaches*, Hodder & Stoughton, 1954.

Churchill, W., *The River War*, NEL Books, 1973.

Churchill, W., *The Second World War*, Vols. II & III, 1985.

Compton-Hall, R., *Submarine Warfare: The Monsters and the Midgets*, Blandford, 1985.

Costello, J. & Hughes, T., *The Battle of the Atlantic*, Fontana, 1980.

Cremer, P., *U333*, Bodley Head, 1984.

Grainger, J. D., 'The Navy in the River Plate', *Mariner's Mirror*, Vol. 81.

Hinsley, F. H. et al., *British Intelligence in the Second World War*, Vol. 2, HMSO, 1981.

Howard Bailey, C., *The Battle of the Atlantic*, Sutton, 1994.

Kahn, D., *Seizing the Enigma*, Souvenir, 1991.

Keegan, J. *A History of Warfare*, Hutchinson, 1993.

Levasseur, J., *Combats sur Mer*, France Empire, 1946.

Lewin, R., *Ultra goes to War*, Hutchinson, 1978.

McKay, J. & Hartland, J., *The Flower Class Corvette AGASSIZ*, Conway, 1993.

Middlebrook, M., *Convoy*, Penguin, 1978.

Milner, M., *North Atlantic Run, The Royal Canadian Navy and the Battle for the Convoys*, Toronto, 1985.

Ministry of Defence, *The U-Boat War in the Atlantic*, 1989.

de Morsier, P., *Les Corvettes de la France Libre*, France Empire, 1972.

Piekalkiewicz, J., *Sea War 1939–1945*, 1987.

Poolman, K., *Sea Hunters. Escort Carriers and U-boats, 1941–45*, Arms & Armour, 1982.

Robertson, T., *Walker R. N.*, Evans, 1956.

Rohwer, J., *The Critical Convoy Battles of March 1943*, Allan, 1977.

Rohwer, J., *Axis Submarine Successes*, Stephens, 1983.

Rohwer, J. & Hümmelchen, G., *Chronology of the War at Sea*, Military Book Society, 1974.

Rusbridger, J., *Who Sank Surcouf?*, Century, 1991.

Schofield, B. B., *The Russian Convoys*, Pan, 1971.

Showell, J. M., *U-Boat Command and the Battle of the Atlantic*, Conway, 1989.

Slader, J., *The Fourth Service. Merchantmen at War 1939–1945*, Hale, 1994.

Williams, M., *Captain Gilbert Roberts R. N. and the Anti-U-Boat School*, Cassell, 1979.

Winser, J. de S., *The D-Day Ships,* The World Ship Society, 1994.

Winton, J., *Ultra at Sea*, Cooper, 1988.

Unpublished sources

ADM & DEFE series at the Public Record Office at Kew, London.

Ruegg, R. A., 'HMS Narcissus, K74' 1991.

U-Boat War Diaries in the Foreign Documents Section of the Ministry of Defence, London.

Index

Air Forces, 23, 47, 51, 56, 109, 117, 122–5, 130–1, 154–5, 184
Asdic, 8, 32, 49, 115, 133
Argentia (Newfoundland), 24–6, 29, 54, 56, 64, 74, 85, 127

Balme, Sub/Lieutenant D. E., RN 39–41
Baker-Cresswell, Commander A. J., RN 14, 39–40
B-Dienst, 97, 131
BNLOs, 13, 30, 32, 119
Boyer, Lieutenant F. L., RN 104
Bridgeman, Commander C. E., RNR 52
Briggs, Chief Petty Officer, RN (the Cox'n), 6, 69
Briggs, Lieutenant H. C. RNVR (HARVESTER), 102
Burial at sea, 103
'Buzzes', 71–2

CAM Ships, 33, 46–8, 160
Captain 'D', Greenock (Captain L. Saunders, RN), 21, 51–2, 81–2, 100–5, 118
Captain 'D', St John's, 142
'Captain' (NARCISSUS), 5, 72–3, 149, 191

Censorship, 67–8
C-in-C, Western Approaches, Admiral Sir Max Horton, 46, 106, 131, 167
Commander U-Boats, Admiral Karl Dönitz, GN, 89, 96, 119, 129–31, 136–7, 139–42
Commmodores RNR, Convoy:
Austin, 64
Bedford, D. M., 65
Birnie, H. C., 53
Boddam-Whetham, E. K., 148, 169
Brooke, J. K., 150, 177
Brownrigg, Sir H., 86
Candy, A. C., 45
Cochrane, Sir E. O., 48, 161
Cocks, A., 148
Davies, Sir A. J., 118
Denis, 59
Dunn, J. O., 95
Fitzmaurice, Sir R., 55, 114
Forsythe, H. C., 79
Fremantle, C. A., 146
Fullerton, Sir E., 80
Goldsmith, M. L., 59, 62
Jones, G. N., 50
Mackenzie, W. B., 45
Mackworth, 47

Magee, W. E. B., 56
Manners, E., 44, 63
Marten, F. A., 159
Moir, D. F., 51
Owen, T. H., 83
Powell, J., 115
Ramsey, Sir C., 169
Rayne, C. N., 127
Taylor, F. H., 64
Thesiger, B. S., 44
Van den Donker, 123
Whitehorn, I. W., 88
Woodward, H., 86
Convoy code and number:
ETM1, 188
ETM5, 189
FTL1, 188
HX145, 44
HX151, 46
HX158, 48
HX165, 50
HX188, 56
HX194, 60
HX202, 62–3
HX207, 64
HX218, 80
HX228, 74, 95–6
HX229, 90
HX232, 115
HX239, 118
HX259, 19, 146
KMS16, 121
L1, 185–7
MKS16, 124
MKS34/SL143, 154
ON9, 44
ON14, 45
ON19, 46
ON40, 49
ON54, 52
ON70, 53

ON121, 62
ON136, 65
ON157, 83
ON174, 113–4
ON208, 148
ONS15, 125
ONS18/ON202, 131–142
ONS26, 47
ONS33, 48
ONS47, 50
ONS60, 53
ONS84, 56
ONS98, 59
ONS126, 63–4
ONS146, 79
ONS160, 86
ONS167, 88–9
OS35, 62
OS49, 121
OS61/KMS35, 150
OS65/KMS39, 156
OS69/KMS43, 161
OS73/KMS47, 177
SC42, 45
SC49, 47
SC56, 49
SC66, 53
SC68, 53–4
SC75, 55
SC106, 65
SC117, 86
SC118, 87–8
SC122, 90
SC143, 147
SC146, 148
SL132, 124
SL147/MKS38, 16, 159–61
SL150,MKS41, 176
SL151/MKS42, 169
SL155/MKS46, 177
Convoy shape, 16–8

Couvade, 69, 151

Coy, Lt/Commander G, RN and Third Officer Barbara Stewart WRNS, 23

Crow's Nest Club (St John's Newfoundland), 26

De Fonbrune, Lieutenant, FFS, 117, 119

De Morsier, Lieutenant P., FFS, 32

Denton (Manchester), 66, 192

Diaries x, 167

Drew, S/Lieutenant G. H., RNVR, 120

'Enigma'/'Ultra', 40–1, 89, 96, 111, 115, 140–2, 147, 155

Edye, Lieutenant R., RNVR, 4, 120, 149

Escort and Support Groups (other than B3):
B1, 12, 105, 124–5
B2, 12, 87
B4, 90, 167
B5, 90
B7, 12, 105, 148
C2, 131
2EG, 108, 159
6EG, 96, 154–6
4SG, 119
7SG, 149, 170
9SG, 131

Evans, Commander M. J., RN, 113, 124–5, 141, 156, 161, 170–5, 178–9

Fisher, Stoker W. A., RCNVR (ST CROIX), 135

Flag Officer, Gibraltar, 124

Flag Officer, Glasgow, 21

'Foxer', 137, 147, 176, 191

Free French Ships:
ACONIT, 31, 49, 66, 79, 83, 88, 95–108, 113, 123, 125, 162–3
ALYSSE, 32, 53
COMMANDANT DETRO-YAT, 49–50, 53
LA DECOUVERT, 170
LOBELIA, 32, 45, 47, 50, 54, 59, 66, 79, 82, 83, 86, 87–8, 131
MIMOSA, 32, 49
RENONCULE, 45, 56, 59, 62, 88, 95, 105, 117, 119, 126, 131, 148, 175
ROSELYS, 79, 83, 88, 95, 104, 117, 131, 142, 162–4
SURCOUF, 29, 30, 32, 104

Geddes, Lieutenant G. C. RNR (AZALEA), 116

German patrol groups ('wolf-packs'):
BORKUM, 156
LERCHE, 115
LEUTHEN, 131
MOSEL, 119
NEULAND, 97–105
PFEIL, 88

German submarines:
U-30, 40
U-31, 46
U-41, 46
U-110, 40
U-168, 115
U-191, 125
U-229, 134
U-238, 160
U-260, 133, 137, 173
U-264, 160

U-270, 10, 133
U-336, 97
U-341, 131
U-424, 160
U-432, 100
U-444, 98
U-501, 46
U-502, 160
U-558, 100
U-563, 115
U-575, 176–7
U-609, 88
U-664, 89
U-666, 138–9
U-706, 116
U-734, 160
U-741, 189
U-752, 119
U-757, 98
U-762, 160
German surface vessels:
ALSTERUFER, 155
ALTMARK, 50
MAGDEBURG, 40
VP2623, 40
Gray, Lieutenant P., RNVR, 4,
120, 149
Greene, Leading Ordnance
Artificer, RN, 68

Hanson, Able Seaman H. E.,
RN (Survivor), 80
Harris, Lieutenant B. W. RNVR
(ORCHIS), 170
Heavy-duty underpants, 76
'Hedgehog' weapon 8, 43, 132,
160, 170, 189
Henderson, Commander H.P.,
RN, 54
His Majesty's Ships (other than
NARCISSUS):

ACTIVITY 159, 162
ANGUILLA, 179
ANCHUSA, 179
ANTELOPE, 46
ARCHER, 119
ASPHODEL, 176–8
AUBRETIA, 39–40
AUDACITY, 85, 96, 106
AZALEA, 113, 116–7
BATTLER, 121
BITER, 60, 149
BEAGLE, 44–6, 49–50, 198
BOADICEA, 44–5, 50–2, 54,
198
BULLDOG, 14, 39–40, 79, 82,
192, 198
CLOVER, 43
CHANTICLEER, 149
COTSWOLD, 186
COWSLIP, 170
CRANE, 149
CURACOA, 73
DIANTHUS, 52
ENTERPRISE, 155
ESCAPADE, 88, 95, 104, 113,
119, 131–2
FENCER, 150
FIREDRAKE, 56, 105
GAMBIA, 121
GEORGETOWN, 80, 84–5
GLADIOLUS, 100, 177
GLASGOW, 155
HARVESTER, 12, 13, 56, 59,
62, 79, 88–9, 95–108
HEATHER, 44, 49–50
HIGHLANDER, 167
HURRICANE, 12, 105, 124–5
ICARUS, 131, 141
ITCHEN, 11, 52, 131, 134–41
KEPPEL, 113, 119, 121, 123–
5, 131, 134, 138

KITE, 148
LAGAN, 131–2
LEEDS CASTLE, 177, 191
LINCOLN, 80
LOCH ALVIE, 149
MAGPIE, 160
MIGNONETTE, 56, 185, 189
NAIRANA, 159, 162
ORLANDO, 14, 101
ORCHIS, 59, 62, 79, 82, 119,
  127, 131, 159, 170, 189
OXLIP, 185, 188
PANSY, a.k.a.
  HEARTSEASE, 11
PHEASANT, 149
POLYANTHUS, 48, 52, 131–
  4, 177
PRIMROSE, 59
PRINCE ROBERT, 150
ROXBOROUGH, 50, 59, 83–
  5, 104
SALISBURY, 44–6
SPARTIATE, 14
STARLING, 108, 159
STRIKER, 154
SWALE, 83, 86
TOWY, 125, 131, 145, 150–1,
  154–5, 159, 161, 170, 178
TUMULT, 121
TWEED, 154
TYRIAN, 121
USK, 149
WATCHMAN, 154
WESTERN ISLES (Tober-
  mory) 41, 67
WHIMBREL, 148
WILDGOOSE, 108, 160
WINCHELSEA, 44
WINDRUSH, 154
WITCH, 63, 86
WOODPECKER, 160

H. M. Trawlers:
  DAMSAY, 186
  DANEMAN, 119
  FUSILIER, 127
  LADY MADELEINE, 49,
    150, 154
  NORTHERN FOAM, 131,
    134, 145, 159
  NORTHERN GEM, 119
  SEAGULL, 45
H. M. Tugs:
  ASSIDUOUS, 150
  BUSTLER, 127
  HESPERIA, 127
  TENACITY, 51
HF/DF, 34, 45, 55, 57, 79, 81,
  89, 96, 111, 115, 132, 135, 160,
  178

Icebergs, 90, 114–5, 118–9
Inspection at sea, 42, 172–5

Jones, Lieutenant T. RNVR, 4,
  120

Kolb-Bernard, Commandant
  FFN, 162–6

Le Millier, Commandant FFN,
  163
Lemp, Kapitanleutnant Julius,
  GN, 39–40
Levasseur, Lieutenant J. FFN,
  98–102
Locusts, 121–2
Lukin-Johnston, Lieutenant D.
  RCNVR, 103

MAC Ships:
  SS. EMPIRE MACALPINE,
    33, 131, 134

SS. EMPIRE MACANDREW, 125
MAGOG, Admiralty yacht, 47
Meeke, Lieutenant H. C. RNVR
Merchant Navy vessels, i.e. 'Steam Ship':
ANDREW F. LUCKEN-BACK, 98
AEGEUS, 53
ATHENIA, 40
ATHOL PRINCE, 79
BALTROVER, 53
BARBARY, 80
BRANT COUNTY, 63, 98
CAVINA, 63
CITY OF ADELAIDE, 115
CORNERBROOK, 59
CRAGPOOL, 53
DORELIAN, 55
DUNNOTTAR CASTLE, 169
EMPIRE HEYWOOD, 155
EURYBATES, 123
EVERLEIGH, 45
F. J. WOLFE, 125
FORT JEMSEG, 136
FRAMLINGTON COURT, 48
FRESNO CITY, 116
GEISHA, 86
HEKTORIA, 44
HENRY BACON, 146
HENRY WYNKOOP, 100, 104
HH ROGERS, 66, 89
JAMAICAN PRODUCER, 73-4, 98
JAMES SMITH, 135
JONATHAN HOLT, 161
JR PARK, 146
KING STEPHEN, 45
LACKENBY, 86
LAWTON EVANS, 98

MADOERA, 151
MANCHESTER EXPORTER, 114
MANCHESTER MER-CHANT 47
MOUNT MYCALE, 86
NIKOLINA MATROVIC, 52
NOAH WEBSTER, 116
OLIGARCH, 121
OREGON EXPRESS, 136
PACIFIC EXPLORER, 51
PACIFIC GROVE, 116-7
PLOMAR, 127
QUEEN MARY (RMS), 73
RANGITATA, 118-9
RARANGA, 50
RENA, 64, 148
RIMUTAKA, 146
ROSARIO, 89
RUAHINE, 127
SAMBUT, 188
SAN TIRSO, 159
SARPEDON, 169
SAUGOR, 45
SCOTTISH TRADER, 50
SHANTUNG, 51, 72
SICILIAN PRINCESS, 44
SKELBRED, 136
SKIENSFJORD, 83
SOBO, 150
STANHOPE, 155
STANLEY MATTHEWS, 146
STEEL VOYAGER, 136
STUYVESANT, 159
SUERTE, 89
TETELA, 95
TILAPA, 56
TUCURINGA, 98, 104
TUNGSHA, 116
ULYSSES, 115-6
VILLE DE TAMATAVE, 86

WALLSEND, 80
WATERLAND, 62
WEARWOOD, 65
WILLIAM G. GORGAS, 98–102
Mers-el-Kebir, 29–30
MONTBRETIA, RNN, 29
Muselier, Admiral FFN, 50

National Maritime Museum (Greenwich), 108–9
Neave, Leading Officers' Steward J., RN, 7
Noble, Admiral Sir P., 120

O'Reilly, S/Lieutenant (E) L. G. RNVR, 149, 183

Polish Navy Ships (ORP):
  BLYSKAWICA, 28, 163
  BURZA, 13, 28, 88–9, 95, 102, 113, 121, 150, 154, 159, 162, 170
  GARLAND, 13, 28, 56, 66, 79–81, 83, 88–9, 95, 108, 119, 198
  PIORUN, 13, 28, 54, 59,62, 170
Rescue Ships (S.S.):
  ACCRINGTON, 113
  BURY, 178
  COPELAND, 50
  DEWSBURY, 52
  GROWLER, 119
  MELROSE ABBEY, 160
  PERTH, 48
  PINTO, 150
  RATHLIN, 53, 55, 88–9
  SAPPER, 150
  TOWARD, 88
  ZAAFAREN, 44–5

ZAMALEK, 47, 109
RDF (Radar), 8, 42, 115, 133–5
Roberts, Captain G. RN, 43, 87
Rohwer, Professor Jürgen, 139
Royal Canadian Navy Ships:
  BURNHAM, 53
  CHAMBLY, 131
  DRUMHELLER, 131
  GATINEAU, 131
  IROQUOIS, 124–5
  KAMLOOPS, 131
  LUNENBURG, 155
  MORDEN, 131
  SACKVILLE, 131, 135
  ST CROIX 131–5
  ST LAURENT, 48
  SNOWBERRY, 155
Royal Fleet Auxiliary FORTOL, 124

St John's (Newfoundland), 26, 54, 80, 83, 145
Senior Officer's valedictory message to Allied ships, 178–9
Slater, S/Lieutenant R. RNVR, 120
Smith, Commander V. F. RNR, 40
Stark, Admiral H. R. USN, 120
Starr, Captain W. B. S. MN, 50
Submarine Tracking Room (Admiralty), 21

Tait, Commander A. A. RN, 56, 59, 64, 81, 83, 87, 95–105
Thompson, Commander G. G. RN, 104

United States Navy Ships:

BOGUE, 24, 96, 105–6, 119, 177

MAYO, 47

PRAIRIE, 24

WOOLSEY, 55

Walker, Captain F. J. RN, 159

Western Approaches Tactical Unit (Liverpool), 43

White, Commander R. T. RN, 46

White, Petty Officer 'Knocker' RN (Chief Boatswain's Mate), 7, 68–9, 73, 151, 173

Whittle, Lt/Commander J. W. RNVR, 185

Women's Royal Naval Service, 22

Zaunkönig, (acoustic torpedo), 130–142, 145, 147, 176

Zigzagging, 72–3